Personalized
LEARNING

Dedicated to Nancy,
Steady and strong

Personalized
LEARNING

STUDENT-DESIGNED PATHWAYS
TO HIGH SCHOOL GRADUATION

JOHN H. CLARKE

FOREWORD BY
JOSEPH DiMARTINO

CORWIN
A SAGE Company

CORWIN
A SAGE Company

FOR INFORMATION:

Corwin
A SAGE Company
2455 Teller Road
Thousand Oaks, California 91320
(800) 233-9936
www.corwin.com

SAGE Publications Ltd.
1 Oliver's Yard
55 City Road
London EC1Y 1SP
United Kingdom

SAGE Publications India Pvt. Ltd.
B 1/I 1 Mohan Cooperative Industrial Area
Mathura Road, New Delhi 110 044
India

SAGE Publications Asia-Pacific Pte. Ltd.
3 Church Street
#10-04 Samsung Hub
Singapore 049483

Copyright © 2013 by Corwin

Printed in the United States of America.

Library of Congress Cataloging-in-Publication Data

A catalog record of this book is available from the Library of Congress.

ISBN: 978-1-4522-5854-6

This book is printed on acid-free paper.

Acquisitions Editor: Arnis Burvikovs
Associate Editor: Desirée A. Bartlett
Editorial Assistant: Mayan N. White
Production Editors: Cassandra Margaret Seibel
    and Melanie Birdsall
Copy Editor: Amy Rosenstein
Typesetter: C&M Digitals (P) Ltd.
Proofreader: Caryne Brown
Indexer: Karen Wiley
Cover Designer: Glenn Vogel
Permissions Editor: Jennifer Barron

Certified Chain of Custody
SUSTAINABLE FORESTRY INITIATIVE
Promoting Sustainable Forestry
www.sfiprogram.org
SFI-01268

SFI label applies to text stock

13 14 15 16 17 10 9 8 7 6 5 4 3 2 1

Contents

Foreword

The audience was paying rapt attention. James was on a small stage in front of a group of twenty teachers, administrators, and community members, including his mother, from Bristol, Vermont. Also in the audience were educators from five other communities across New England. Despite what should be a nerve-wracking situation for a struggling ninth grader, he was coolly and calmly explaining the musical history that led to the evolution of the modern electric guitar. It was his public exhibition for course credit earned through the Pathways program at Mount Abraham Union High School.

His passion for music led to this event. He was clearly thrilled to be able to build a guitar of his own as part of his schooling. His pride in his work was evident.

After explaining the history of the guitar, he proceeded to focus on the science of sound waves. It was a deep discussion of sound waves. Again, everyone was impressed. I was thinking that James must be a strong student.

James then proceeded to show his progress in making a guitar. This was the passion that opened the door for him to earn half credits over a semester—one each in science, history, and art.

The most compelling part of James's exhibition came during the public comment session at the end of his hour's presentation. His teary-eyed mom publicly thanked his advisor and the others involved in the Pathways program for giving her back her son. She explained that James had been struggling in his relationship with school and, more poignantly, with how that difficult relationship had clouded the bond between mother and son.

This was a moving moment for me. After decades of trying to assist schools to meet the needs of all students, I was on this day presented with a strong vision of how schools should be different in a way that meets the needs of all students and their families.

In this book, John Clarke explains how an entire community—youth and adults, students, teachers, mentors, community groups, business owners, and parents—is transforming its high school by creating a personalized learning experience for its youth.

It paints a picture of how a personalized high school might look using the words of those who created it. It asks readers to listen to the voices of students, advisors, administrators, and community members to describe their individual experiences in the development of a personalized high school. These stories show how personalizing learning provides deep learning by all youth.

In the current public discussion, *personalizing* is often interpreted as *online learning* in which students interact with computers to learn. The Pathways program has learned that online resources can be valuable as part of larger projects. But online courses cannot provide the level of deep understanding that students at the Pathways program have demonstrated.

Learning is always personal because it depends on personal curiosity, effort, practice, and persistence. Personalized learning engages students in using information to manage their lives and to participate actively in their communities. James's story at Pathways illustrates a failure of conventional classes and a return to active learning in a community setting. Personalized learning is not a linear process; it is circular, recursive, self-adjusting, and increasingly complex, preparing students to manage change in their lives and the lives of others.

There are three compelling aspects of this book:

1. It lets students, advisors, community mentors, and administrators speak in their own voices about personalized learning.

2. It illustrates high school transformation by focusing on one school working through redesign;

3. It includes examples of materials that support independent learning, with a large number of graphics that represent learning processes.

This book provides a convincing road map for educating all of America's students. It is a must-read for anyone who cares about educating all our youth.

Joseph DiMartino, President
Center for Secondary School Redesign, Inc.

Preface

WHY THIS BOOK?

The purpose of this book is to show that a medium sized comprehensive high school can personalize learning while preparing all students to meet common graduation standards. The book aims to inspire readers to consider personalized learning as a feasible approach to secondary reform at a time when the population is growing increasingly diverse, preparation for work has become a high priority, and technology has created access for students to an unlimited amount of useful information. To show that personalization offers a feasible way to redesign secondary learning, I have depended on illustrations from Mount Abraham Union High School in Bristol, Vermont, where such a transformation has been under way for several years. With illustrations in view, I aim to show teachers, administrators, parents, and community members that high school transformation toward personalized learning, Grades 7–12, can happen when the students' personal interests, talents, and aspirations provide a starting point for designing their own pathways toward graduation, work, and college.

This is not an expository text that tells educators how to personalize their schools. My experience suggests that personalizing a high school cannot follow prescriptions. School transformation is a process of growth, following patterns set by earlier growth. Like personalized learning itself, it has to be a process of exploration undertaken by a whole community based more on personal commitment and collegial relationships than on techniques. Mount Abe's personalization initiative proves that transformation is possible, even in an old institution that has defied a long list of alternative ideas. I have used the term *high school* referring to any secondary school, Grades 6–12.

Unlike research studies or personal narratives about secondary learning, this book should accomplish the following:

- Spark the imagination of people who want more students to succeed in in secondary schools, Grades 6–12
- Illustrate the feasibility of developing customized curricula for students with highly distinctive orientations to learning
- Demonstrate how secondary schools can increase their effectiveness by opening access to knowledge from widely diverse sources in a community
- Describe how new roles can expand professional options for teachers when students take more control over their own learning

A comprehensive high school can help *all students* prepare for work, college, and adult roles if the school organizes itself to serve *each student*, one at a time.

WHO MIGHT READ THIS BOOK?

Because parents, students, educators, and community members play essential parts in school transformation, I hope readers from across the broad network that supports public education will use this book to consider new ways to engage young adults in learning. Because educators have the primary responsibility for making schools work, of course—and because adapting their professional roles is essential—I see teachers and administrators making up most of the readership, with students preparing to become innovative educators in the mix as well. Most profoundly, I hope high school students see the book as a way to confirm their sense that school can be different from what it has been for so long—increasing their willingness to take leading roles in their own education. Personalization is the work of a whole community, which might benefit the most if all participants read these stories simultaneously while in conversation with each other.

WHAT'S IN THE BOOK?

Despite the uniformity prescribed by curriculum guides, each of us would tell a unique story about how and what we learned in high school; a book about personalized learning has to begin with personal stories that are told from many different viewpoints. Rather than obsess about theory, I have chosen to let the students, advisors, mentors, parents, and administrators tell their own stories, describing their own experience with personalized learning. Then I have tried to weave their stories into a comprehensible fabric of connected ideas in each chapter. You will not find any ultimate prescriptions here. You may find, instead, a story that encourages growth from within, showing how a conventional high school can create a new version of itself because students come to school actively engaged in creating new versions of themselves. Interactions among adults and students at Mount Abraham drive the process of school transformation, as people who come to share the same vision enact specific changes and develop new roles—the best means I know for making change happen at the secondary level.

I gathered ideas and transcribed stories from interviews conducted over a 3-year period at Mount Abraham, during which I was also a consultant to the faculty, a community mentor, and a volunteer advisor. With adults and Pathways students, I used the same focusing questions to organize wide-ranging conversations.

What are you working on right now?

How did your work get to this point?

What led you to consider personalized pathways to graduation?

With minimal cutting and editing, I have tried to preserve the "voice" of those I interviewed and reveal the larger scope of their stories. Rather than presenting short clips illustrating isolated concepts, I tried to capture the creative turmoil that arises when many students simultaneously design personal pathways to high school graduation and explore distinctive futures in the adult world. In these stories, their work will appear unique, but their sense of personal efficacy will stand out.

Unusual stories of personal accomplishment have propelled the evolution toward personalization at Mount Abraham for 15 years, long before Pathways began to integrate related programs, then expanded from independent studies, to a full-time option for some students, to a variable credit option for all students organized within the Department of Personalized Learning, which then helped shape a whole-school transformation initiative. Mount Abraham students have told stories of their learning projects at school board meetings, in public exhibitions in the town hall, and at regional conferences, often receiving expressions of acclaim and wonder. Within the school district, they have enlisted their parents in project development or worked with a wide variety of community mentors on learning projects, gradually weaving a fabric of legends that slowly expanded the community's hopes for its high school. With the stories, I have included illustrations from Pathways learning guides, showing how personalized learning can be designed so all students move toward different goals. I have also referred briefly to research from earlier efforts to engage all students, particularly studies of separate aspects of personalization that high schools can organize into a coherent process that supports learning for each student, one at a time.

Acknowledgments

No individual had envisioned the Pathways process in its current form. Instead, school transformation at Mount Abraham is emerging through interactions across the institutional lines that usually divide education into fiefdoms—academic departments, administrative offices, special education services, counseling, and student services. The Pathways team, made up of the following individuals, has contributed to the development of this book:

- Russell Comstock, a community advisor with a special interest in global issues and experiential learning
- Maureen Deppman, social studies teacher supporting independent projects and a Middle School Pathways Exploratory course
- Gerrie Heuts, the far-ranging community liaison who finds internships and conducts rolling seminars on car trips throughout the county
- Josie Jordan, an English teacher with broad experience in communication and the arts
- Vicki Buffalo, an advisor with extensive experience with students at risk of failure
- Caroline Camara, team leader, advisor, former chemistry teacher, and member of the Mount Abraham transformation team
- Lauren Parren, coordinator of technology for the school district, including the online student portfolios and standards-based transcripts used at Pathways

You will hear from the members of the school community, who have also been actively engaged in developing Pathways and Personalized Learning: community mentors, who sponsor Pathways kids in their work settings; coprincipals Andy Kepes and Leon Wheeler, who lead the school transformation team, weaving small initiatives into a larger fabric; Nancy Cornell, Associate Superintendent for Curriculum, who wrestles with the intricacies of district-level change; Evelyn Howard, our Superintendent of Schools, who has organized policy development and has led the school boards to see how personalized learning meets the needs of this community; and Armando Vilaseca, Vermont's Secretary of Education, who has been deeply involved deeply in statewide efforts to engage students in learning and to make room in the system for change.

I particularly want to acknowledge all the students who recounted their stories for this book, whose courage and energy have pushed back the limits of what we think is possible. The Metropolitan Career and Technical Center—the Met—in Providence, Rhode Island, provided much of the inspiration and structure for Pathways at Mount Abraham by hosting a visit, offering materials, and illustrating how a personalized high school might look. Through Big Picture Learning in Providence, Rhode Island, the Met version of personalization has spread through more than 80 secondary schools in the United States, including three new Big Picture Schools in Vermont and more than 40 schools internationally (http://www.bigpicture.org/about-us/). The New Country School in Henderson, Minnesota, hosted the Pathways design team and demonstrated a workable and inspiring structure for project-based learning. For examples of skills assessment rubrics, the team went to the Compass School in southeastern Vermont. Other models and ideas arrived over the Internet and telephone.

The support of the Nellie Mae Foundation provided initial funding for Pathways, helping energize the long process of high school transformation at Mount Abraham, as it has throughout the Northeast. For an inspiring vision of high schools adapting to the modern world, please consider reading Sir Kenneth Robinson's *The element: How finding your passion changes everything* (London: Penguin), and watching his videos.

PUBLISHER'S ACKNOWLEDGMENTS

Corwin would like to thank the following individuals for their editorial insight and guidance:

Sara Coleman, Science Instructor
Norwalk High School
Norwalk, IA

Dr. Patricia Conner, Curriculum
Berryville Public Schools
Berryville, AR

Dr. Gary Frye
Homeless Liaison / Grant Writer & Executive Director
Lubbock-Cooper ISD & Llano Estacado Rural Communities
Foundation
Lubbock, TX

Dr. Kathy Grover, Assistant Superintendent
Clever R-V Public Schools
Clever, MO

Mary Beth Hamel, Assistant Superintendent
Ayer Shirley Regional School District
Ayer, MA

Deborah A. Langford, School Counselor
West Hills Elementary STEM Academy
Bremerton, WA

Dr. Cathy Patterson, Grade 5 Teacher
Walnut Valley Unified School District
Walnut, CA

Dr. Judith Rogers, K–5 Mathematics Specialist
Tucson Unified School District
Tucson, AZ

About the Author

 **John H. Clarke** began teaching high school English in Massachusetts in 1966. He moved to Vermont in 1977 to prepare secondary teachers, interact with local high schools, and run a teaching improvement program for faculty at the University of Vermont. He joined the research team in the Secondary Initiative at Brown University's Education Alliance and Lab at Brown (LAB), focusing on student engagement and high school personalization. Often with others, he has written or edited several books and many articles, focusing on thinking strategies, personalization, high school change, high school teaching, and systems adaptation. Four of those books focus on personalized learning:

Engaging Each Student: Personalized Learning in Secondary School Reform (2008)

Personalized Learning: Preparing High School Students to Create Their Futures (2006)

Personalized Learning: Personal Learning Plans, Portfolios and Presentations (2004)

Personalized Learning: An Introduction (2003)

He helped create a system of professional development schools in Vermont, linking teacher preparation and school improvement. For more than 20 years, he has worked to engage all students with the faculty and staff at Mount Abraham Union High School, where he now volunteers with the Pathways Team, designing personalized pathways to graduation with students who want to manage their own learning.

Introduction

All Learning
Is Personal

W hen I was teaching high school English, I began to see
a distressing pattern in my seating chart; similar students seemed to cluster in the same sectors of the room every class period, forming very small neighborhoods in a crowded space. The "Class Map" (Figure I.1) shows the general pattern. From my lonely vigil at the front, I could often hear the socialites, droning like bees in the center of the room. As much as I may have wanted to expunge their joyful chatter, the waving hands of a few overachievers in the front row usually prevented me from making much contact, almost as if the socialites had planned it that way. Over by the windows sat the poets, entranced by their private visions. Behind them, a huddle of dreamers gazed mournfully out the windows, traveling in their heads to foreign shores. A crew of cynics glowered from behind the socialites, perhaps hiding their math homework behind our huge literature textbook, which I tried not to notice. Outcasts scattered themselves in lonely isolation on the darker side of the room. I learned not to worry about the outcasts, who would probably not risk making a public display of their uneasy status. The escapists entered the room last and left as soon as possible. I could barely see the underachievers slumped down in their seats—out of view—which was part of their plan, anyway. Leaning against the back wall,

a squad of snipers lay waiting for the appearance of some laughable frailty. And the outlaws, well, they didn't show up often enough to make a difference—except in short, dramatic bursts. All learning is personal, and my students were personally distinctive.

These tiny neighborhoods offered their citizens protection—from other neighborhoods and from me. Entrenched behind their customary desks, they faced the same assignments, took the same tests, and arranged themselves smoothly on the same grading scale, but they were wildly different people. Most high school classes, even in English, have been designed to convey a defined body of knowledge and an array of skills to all students at once, as if they were passive receptacles identical in their interests, talents, and aspirations. What

| Figure I.1 | Class Map: Natural Distribution of Students in My Classroom |

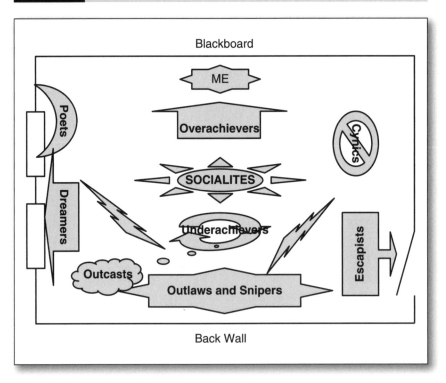

galvanizing challenge can any teacher cook up to engage them all simultaneously?

Struggling to avoid shameful incidents, most of my students worked hard to open a gulf of impersonal distance between themselves and English literature—and me—the same strategy they had adopted more generally to survive throughout our large, impersonal school. But learning cannot be impersonal. It occurs through personal effort and requires personal energy. We commit personal effort only to tasks we believe are important. Responding to a challenge we regard as personally important, we ask questions, gather information, acquire skills, envision good results, and try different tactics to get closer to results we desire. When we face a real challenge to our hopes and beliefs, learning helps reduce tension and promises some satisfaction. Learning engages our attention and even offers moments of personal joy. It is always purposeful. Learning requires action; high schools reward passivity. Since high school students are unique unto themselves, broadcasting information across a roomful of young faces produces uneven results. Students tend to organize themselves into patterns that better support acquiescence and conformity than engagement.

MEETING STANDARDS/AVOIDING STANDARDIZATION

Moving all students through the same sequence of years, each about 180 days in length, and through four to nine class periods each day, we aim to produce uniformity in the results we achieve—high levels proficiency for all. But we do not get uniform results, particularly in test scores. Instead, we get a pattern of achievement that resembles the bell curve we are trying to replace with high standards for all. Despite an enormous investment in testing since *A Nation at Risk* (National Commission on Excellence in Education, 1983), some students score high because they have always scored high. Some students "hold down the tail" of the bell curve, and they have always scored at that level. A great bulge of students in the murky middle seems to defy our understanding. They respond idiosyncratically to tasks and tests. After 20 years of standards-based reform, we have not changed the curve. If all the inputs have been similar but we get a predictable pattern of achievement in the results, it may be that students decide whether they want to achieve at high levels—or not. They are not uniform, so they do not respond the same way to what we do. Each one is uniquely oriented to the pursuit of personal interests. Tests ignore personal interests and achievements that cannot be put on a comparative scale, one student against another.

Test scores do not serve the purpose of helping students improve their performance. If you look at Friday's quiz scores, semester grade reports, international TIMSS (Trends in International Mathematics and Science Study) scores, SATs, or statewide proficiency tests, the same pattern persists—high, middle, and low. Stated crudely, when we cast the same body of knowledge across a great, diverse pool of talent, interest, and aspiration, we get the same disappointing distribution of results, and that distribution means that we have not succeeded in reaching all the kids. Decades of test scores demonstrate that a standardized approach does not affect all students the same way, no matter how long or hard we push. We can extend the school day, shorten summers, and remove everything but core subjects from the curriculum, but doing the same things harder and longer does not change the basic pattern

CELEBRATING DIVERSITY

Standardized tests are not designed to highlight the special talents and aspirations that individuals bring to the fluidity of social need. Over the millennia, our burgeoning species has accumulated a multitude of capabilities that we may or may not need to meet immediate challenges that assail our culture. Learning within a culture must be wide and broad enough to ensure that we are ready for unforeseeable changes, both threats and opportunities. A wide array of uniquely accomplished individuals—including artists, mechanics, engineers, tea-growers, birders, bikers, and ballplayers—can ensure that humanity can adapt to flux in the environment. For a society to thrive, continual adaptation is the key. Freezing all secondary schools into a single model restricts adaptive change and practically guarantees obsolescence of skills and knowledge. Demanding the same results for all students in a school restricts their growth as well.

We are fortunate in not producing graduates with identical skills and knowledge because our society could not employ that many engineers, auto mechanics, designers, or marketing specialists. The health of the society depends on maintaining a steady flow of uniquely talented young people into an enormous array of career and life options that demand different kinds of educational preparation and experience—and that are changing much faster than our education system. Limiting the purpose of secondary schools to high math, science, social studies, and English test scores cannot generate the range of skills and knowledge we need to thrive as a society or as a species. Standardized testing masks the capabilities that we should recognize, develop, and celebrate. Expecting uniform results among people who are not the same and who plan to remain distinctive guarantees a persistent pattern of failure. As a species, we have to adapt to survive. But we have to learn, one of us at a time, to convert individual interests, hopes, and talents into distinctive strengths. Personalized high school learning allows those strengths to develop from within the local and global communities that need them.

Rather than seeking high test scores on a few scales, we would do better by teaching the skills of successful adaptation to ongoing change—gathering and organizing information, resolving complex problems, communicating, or creating novel products useful to ourselves and others—and working with others from a diverse population to improve our condition. Early civilizations, we hear in ninth-grade world history courses, nurtured four social roles: farming to produce food for the group, soldiering to protect it, priesthood to predict and guide its future, and parenthood to produce the future. For most of human history, educating the young for these roles occurred by way of *internship,* hands-on practice with a skilled adult. Now we have innumerable roles to fill, with more appearing daily, and we are still treating students as if they are preparing for the same future and should learn for the same purpose. To succeed with all students, we need to start with the interests each one brings to school, and then direct some of their personal energy toward a few common goals, enabling all of them to work together to shape a culture we cannot imagine from where we sit, caught in this brief moment between past and future. We have to learn, one of us at a time, to convert our individual interests, hopes, and talents into distinctive strengths and commitments that serve ourselves and our communities.

PERSONALIZED LEARNING

Personalized Learning is a blended approach to learning that combines the delivery of education both within and beyond the traditional classroom environment. The Personalized Learning model fosters a collaborative partnership between the teacher, parent, student and school that designs a tailored learning program for each student according to the needs and interests of each individual student.

—Personalized Learning Foundation

Personalized learning is certainly not new to the educational scene. Individual education plans (IEPs) became the law for special education students decades ago, based on student needs identified through testing. But personalization is not the same as individualization. Personal learning requires the active direction of the student; individualization lets adults tailor the curriculum to scaled assessments of interest and abilities. The difference between individualization and personalization lies in control. We can individualize education by imposing it, but students choose to personalize their own learning. Their volition drives their inquiry. Personal learning plans (PLPs), unlike IEPs, are based on individual strengths and are directed by student choice. Personalized secondary schools use PLPs as an organizing framework that can then incorporate project-based learning, inquiry learning, collaborative learning, tutoring, advisories, writing to learn, and other strategies that promote personal engagement.

A personalized high school is accountable for building a coherent and effective process of support for personal inquiry; students are accountable for doing the work and producing results demonstrating their competency in a few crucial areas. The learning is personal, but assessment is public. Personalized learning lets us and our students seize opportunities for growth that fit both deepening interests and trends in the flow of societal change. Personalized learning is active learning, organized so students learn to answer questions they see as important to their lives. Because students learn to gather information to solve problems they recognize in their own experience, personalized learning is often called "authentic," mirroring the processes adults use to solve problems at work, at home, or in a community. Guided by skilled teachers, students look carefully at what they know, generate questions or set goals, gather more information, then use critical thinking skills to propose solutions and present new ideas to an audience of adults and peers. In all these activities, the student is the center of the action, winning praise and eliciting advice from the students, teachers, parents, and community members who witness demonstrations of competency. Personalized learning prepares students to dig deeply into information from many sources, including experience in the community, so they become increasingly adept at managing their minds and their work.

Unlike travel to a distant city, mapping a personal pathway cannot be done once and then followed to the predetermined destination. Any amount of meaningful learning can quickly change both the destination and the route. Distinctive personal pathways emerge through the interaction of students, teachers, community mentors, and, most prominently, advisors who work to ensure learning remains

- flexible rather than rigid,
- dynamic rather than static,
- embedded rather than segregated,
- guided rather than directed,
- mediated rather than transmitted,
- distinctive rather than comparative,
- practical as well as abstract, and
- organized around strengths rather than weaknesses.

In personalized learning, the evidence of learning has to be valid to the audience of students, teachers, parents, and community members who view it.

Personalized learning must be designed to be adaptive, flexing both to the variety of student interests and to needs and opportunities in the surrounding community. Personalized learning does not aim for a static level of achievement. Instead, it encourages continuous refinement of knowledge and skill as the student takes on challenges of increasing complexity. High school students do not find it easy to shift their effort from content acquisition to a self-correcting cycle of growth, but they can make the shift with the support of experienced adults and other students trying to learn the same process. They may come to school as a group but learn to use their minds well "one kid at a time" (Littky, 2005).

In its current form, the Personalized Learning Department and Pathways at Mount Abraham serve multiple purposes:

- Guide course selection and planning
- Help students imagine their future
- Connect families student learning
- Clarify graduation requirements
- Plan a path after high school
- Prepare for college applications

- Celebrate student achievement

- Explore adult roles

- Connect each student with a caring adult

- Promote reflection and reevaluation

- Relate student learning to standards

- Improve learning skills

- Explore noncurricular options

- Explore career choices

- Support identity formation

- Demonstrate personal talents

- Initiate lifelong learning

- Extend range of choice

- Increase self-awareness

- Increase content acquisition

- Emphasize applications of knowledge

- Legitimate nonschool achievements

- Focus on important ideas

- Establish "best-work" portfolio

- Challenge each student

- Engage students in inquiry

- Link skills and knowledge to life

- Help students meet standards

- Increase technological literacy

- Engage each student in learning

- Improve communication skills

- Encourage reflection and adaptation

- Teach problem solving

- Increase cooperation among students

- Strengthen student/faculty relations

- Emphasize shared purpose

- Reduce isolation and alienation

- Link content learning to application

- Increase student motivation

- Reduce anonymity

To simplify this overwhelming list of purposes, personalized learning at Mount Abraham aims to prepare students to communicate, think critically and creatively, participate in the community, collaborate productively with others, and take responsibility for their own growth—the Mount Abraham Graduation Competencies.

Designing Personal Pathways to Graduation

Developing Pathways at Mount Abraham began when a design team of two teachers and two community members set out a basic framework for a pilot semester, funded by the Nellie Mae Foundation, which the current Pathways team continues to design and refine. Quickly, further ideas for redesign came from collaboration among students, teachers, advisors, administrators, and members of the community working together. By far, the most active collaborators have proven to be students and their advisors, who used their relationships to hammer out a detailed conception of personalized learning that outlines fairly reliable steps for a flexible process that accommodates individual interests. Though the adults in the two Pathways rooms have been educated within academic specialties, they work as a team. Each knows all the students, and together they fashion a rich environment that makes independent inquiry possible. The team meets weekly to adjust the program structure and daily to talk about students who need support, Semester by semester, they redesign parts of the process so all students can succeed. The "Pathways Ladder" in Figure I.2 represents the basic structure of a semester as a student progresses toward graduation.

Preparing students to pursue personal interests while meeting graduation standards became the purpose of Pathways, to help students design their own road to a diploma, clarifying their interests and gathering knowledge and applicable skills for the lives they begin to envision. As the program grew in the school, however, it raised a larger

Figure I.2   Pathways Ladder

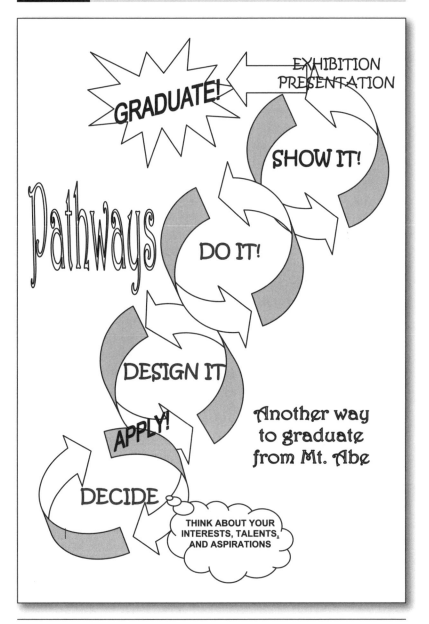

Source: Reprinted with permission from Mount Abraham Union Middle High School, Bristol, Vermont

question: "What if all students learned to choose their way through their high school experience, not in one heroic stab, the way some college sophomores choose a major, but in incremental steps, year by year, semester by semester, week by week and day by day—with the guidance of caring adults?" Pathways helped raise that question, and then opened the question of personalization throughout the high school. "What if?" became "Why not try?" The Personalized Learning Department has become a research and development center, and the graduation competencies, inquiry process, and project formats are being adapted for use in conventional courses.

Pathways students can work toward graduation by completing projects rather than courses. The road to graduation is unique to each student, following a track that no one can predict at the outset but that grows increasingly clear as the student completes projects and designs new ones. Successful projects usually depend on a network of support that connects the family, school, and local community to each student's learning path, thereby enhancing the student's ability to realize dreams and achieve goals in meaningful and relevant ways. But a personalized pathway also includes formal courses chosen by students to build background knowledge and skills—within the school, in local colleges, at the county's vocational center, in specialized training programs, or in virtual form on the Internet. The mix of classes and projects changes each semester as students learn more about themselves and their futures. The assortment of personalized student projects at Pathways and the Personalized Learning Department have been pushing back the boundaries of what the community expects of its high school and its students and how it thinks about education.

Success in Pathways depends directly on student initiative and willingness to try new things, working in concert with the surrounding community of supportive adults. Rather than sitting in classes, they have to move actively toward their interests. Instead of relying on a common schedule, they schedule their own time. The program does not isolate students from their friends or community but instead serves as a gateway to educational opportunities throughout this small rural community. Pathways depends on PLPs, advisors, community mentors, project-based learning, internships, the Internet, standards-based portfolios, quarterly exhibitions of progress, and the five essential competencies. These props and guides are detailed in greater depth in the sections that follow.

Students who choose to direct their learning need a coach, who is referred to as an advisor. Advisors help students translate interests into credits by way of guidelines in student websites, but most advising focuses on personal goals and projects. Pathways advisors help students pursue their interests: clarifying their questions exploring research, building projects in the local area, accessing the Internet, and interacting with community experts, all of which produce evidence of learning they reorganize and revise for exhibitions and electronic portfolios. Advisors focus on one student at a time and prepare all to meet graduation competencies in ways consistent with the directions they have set for their work. Most important, the advisors help students find a place in the community where they can work or design an internship, with support from their parents, friends, high school teachers, and others. Through engagement, students at Pathways learn how to manage their time productively, to assume responsibility for their own progress, and to take themselves seriously as emerging adults.

The Pathways team continues to design and refine its processes, in large part because students, teachers, advisors, administrators, and members of the community must solve problems together, working around student projects. The most active collaborators have proven to be students and their advisors, who used, and still use, their relationships to hammer out a coherent framework for personalized learning that creates defined steps for accommodating individual interests while developing competency against common standards. Students began to refer to their personalized curriculum as "rubber"—a flexible process for learning that prepared each of them to develop personal strengths, interests, and aspirations as they moved toward graduation. Haltingly, the first groups of Pathways students began shaping the culture of their new program. The culture would congeal only when each student had a story to tell that would help the whole group shape the evolution of shared ideas.

AN ENRICHED CONTEXT FOR LEARNING

The Personalized Learning space at Mount Abraham has no desks. Without rows that put some kids behind others or cluster small groups of friends behind defensive bulwarks, students and their advisors spread themselves around two connected classrooms to complete the tasks that mark their personal pathways to graduation (see Figure I.3). No computers stand idle, as kids search for information or devise parts of their exhibitions. The telephones get a workout, particularly as a semester opens the door to new opportunities in the surrounding community. Advisors move from student to student, checking on progress or talking. Open tables create flexible surfaces for projects or small discussions, often led by students. Kids flop on the couch to take breaks. Community mentors, special educators, parents, counselors, and district administrators move easily in and out. A whiteboard waits, ready for practice presentations or the real thing. Students come and go as classes or community mentorships draw them out into larger realms. The room has been designed to support connections between people and information.

I do not believe personalized learning will replace classroom-based learning, nor do I think it should. Most Pathways students include formal classes as they pursue their unique purposes. Students interested in a field of study such as literature, history, or philosophy—where discussion may be essential to learning—might include many formal courses in their plans. Mathematics and science classes will remain prerequisites for some professional studies. At Pathways, all kinds of projects have provided learning experiences for

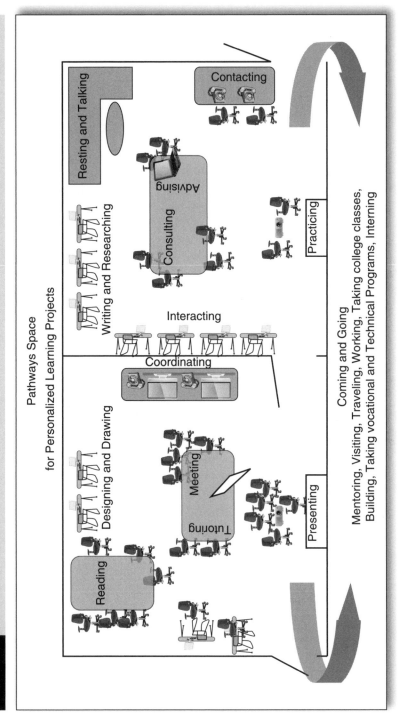

Pathways Space
for Personalized Learning Projects

Source: Reprinted with permission from Mount Abraham Union Middle High School, Bristol, Vermont

15

young people. But Pathways and the Personalized Learning Department do not award credit for experience; they award credit for the products students create, showing they have met standards in communication, critical thinking/problem solving, global citizenship, collaboration, and personal development/ independent learning. Knowledge has exploded in every academic field. Recognizing the ubiquity of accessible knowledge from many sources, it is time for high schools to prepare students to contend with quantities of information, managing their own learning, directing their growth, and improving life in their communities.

1

Engagement in Learning

At Pathways, you can't wait for things to happen. You have to make things happen.

—Student to student

OVERVIEW

Students become engaged in learning when they recognize that they are:

- building skills they will use to fulfill their personal hopes as adults;
- asking and answering questions about how to achieve their goals;
- building on their established strengths and interests; and
- facing meaningful rather than artificial challenges.

Although most students have a natural proclivity toward engagement, they have to learn how to manage complex strategies to fulfill their hopes. Although research on personalized

17

high school learning is scant, related research from the "smaller schools" initiative is promising.

ORGANIZING CURRICULUM AROUND PERSONAL COMPETENCIES

Content-area learning begins with facts, concepts, and processes that govern an academic discipline. Aiming to initiate a process of deep inquiry, personalized learning begins with questions that students ask, at whatever point the student has interest, and then follows a track that unfolds as they take one step after another. Personalized inquiry cannot be taught; it has to be learned as a flexible, self-correcting process that a student can understand and manage. Fenway High School in Boston makes this kind of learning central to the ninth-grade curriculum, but students practice flexible thinking over four years. Focusing on 21st century skills and knowledge, they:

- Are confident that they can learn
- Make accurate assessments of why they succeed in learning
- Think clearly about inaccuracies when failure occurs during tasks
- Actively seek to expand their repertoire of strategies for learning
- Match strategies to the learning task, making adjustments when necessary
- Ask for guidance from peers or the teacher
- Take time to think about their thinking
- View themselves as continual learners and thinkers (North Central Regional Educational Laboratory, 2003; http://atc21s.org/index.php/about/what-are-21st-century-skills/)

Learning to manage mental work happens most easily when students discover a personal interest and pursue it, giving themselves up to the search. Personalized learning does not closely resemble current high school learning—where right answers proliferate as knowledge explodes but probing questions and speculative answers are harder to find.

At Pathways recently, the heat was rising. Exhibitions had been scheduled for the week before students' Christmas break. Students had been glued to their computers all morning, organizing the evidence they would need to earn credit. But as the day grew older, conversation grew steadily. Advisors and students talked passionately about what a project might mean. The superintendent stopped by to make an appointment and sit in with a group of kids critiquing other kids. A school principal met with Caroline and Maureen on their upcoming class, Middle School Pathways Exploratory for seventh-grade students. The security officer looked in, offered a student a job teaching archery, and left. A passing teacher stopped to talk. An advisory group ate cookies happily in the next room. A parent with her daughter and teacher had their heads bent over a project. No one seemed to pay attention to the merry hubbub, and few noticed that the morning break had begun. Then, to my delight, I saw at the central table a cluster of five or six students huddled around a chessboard. A scholarly physics enthusiast and a wild goose specialist sat on one side of the table, and a prospective politician sat on the other. One observer who designs computer games was giving advice three moves ahead of the current array of pieces on the board—for both sides. In the surrounding crowd, the physics enthusiast gave advice on battlefield tactics to a firefighter and a ninth-grade house designer, who argued alternative strategies from her perspective. Together, they all were learning to play chess as an ad hoc team of six divergent minds in one place.

At moments such as these, the Pathways rooms hum with human activity. Individuals carry out their work or talk with others, cluster around a computer, check in with an advisor, then change groups to start another task. In an ordinary classroom, the tenor of the two personalized learning rooms might appear chaotic, because no single subject gathers the attention of all and no individual takes charge of time or space.

Remarkably, when the space boils with energy, what some call "popcorn," work continues uninterrupted because engaged people focus intensely on their tasks. Learning occurs within each of us separately, pushed forward by interactions across the lines that divide us. Interactions drive personalized learning.

Advisors continually provoke students to ask deeper questions as student projects develop. With complex questions, no single answer can end the quest. Caroline Camara, team leader for Pathways and cochair of the Personalized Learning Department, had migrated from bench chemistry to science teaching after several years. Celebrated as the outstanding teacher of the year, she then migrated from team teaching and a multitude of extracurricular groups to Pathways, looking for ways to engage these disengaged students:

> Kids need to be engaged. When that's not there, they don't care about their work—and they don't do it. We have Tyler out at a farm, working almost full time. He comes to school for math, but most of the time he is out there and I have been hearing that he really gets what he is doing and knows how he can process it at school. We have evidence that he can process it at school. He came in with special needs and took a special reading test; his comprehension was right on, but his vocabulary was horrible. So, we put it back on Tyler. What are we going to do to work on vocabulary? He thought for a while, and then he said, "I can text it with Dave, the reading school's specialist."
>
> Dave gave him his first five vocabulary words and said, "Please write five sentences back to me, using these very disparate words, showing me what each one means. Instead of that, Tyler texted back a coherent paragraph using all those words, but relating them back to what he does on the farm every day. He is doing what he is doing. It means something to him. And he is taking this external input and turning it into something that means something to him. It is a testament to his using the tools that he is

comfortable using these days to get a job done. "That's how I am going to do it," he said. "My phone is on me every day. So text me. When I have a minute, I will do it." That's a magical story of engagement.

Somewhat strangely, engaged learning is both the process and outcome of personalized learning. The problem with classroom learning is that the same questions do not engage all students equally. For most, questions they regard as meaningful can lead them to think with focused effort and accept challenges, at the cost of their energy and time. Because they may have had little practice with focused inquiry in their high school classes, students in personalized programs need time to learn how to ask questions and to put productive energy into constructing workable answers.

REAL QUESTIONS/REAL MEANING

I have begun to feel that the questions that matter in high school are always personal—rarely just academic. A group of several individuals could easily launch different questions about the same topic and conduct different inquiries based on different experiences in the community. Some might launch large questions from concern about the human condition: "Will our country become authoritarian?" But most high school students start with questions directly connected to their lives and interests: "Can I learn to live off the land?" "Can I design a perfect house?" "What does it take to become a music producer?" Some might want to expand a vision of themselves: Am I really an artist? Others might want a glimpse of their own future: "What does it take to be a lawyer?" "Can I start my own business?" Whether broad or narrow, the questions student see as "real" force them to look for answers across the subject areas that divide high schools into academic departments and to develop meaningful answers by weaving interdisciplinary threads into useful fabric. "Real problems" and their solutions are almost always interdisciplinary.

In grouping students by subject areas, we are making questionable assumptions about why students put effort into thinking and learning. We may think that quiz scores will inspire inquiry, but many students do not imagine a future in which quiz scores will make a difference. Semester grades may be a personal interest of college-bound students but not to students who cannot imagine going to college—perhaps 50 percent of the population. Scores on standardized tests may inspire personal effort among students who do well on tests, but not among those who do not—and who have felt shame all their lives. We reward students who comply with rules, but some young people spurn conformity, taking a rebellious posture even under benign conditions. We reward competition, but competition usually produces more losers than winners, and the losers learn to back away from games they think they cannot win. Even the prospect of high school graduation does not carry much weight among students for whom high school learning is meaningless and irrelevant—who drop out at rates hovering around 30 percent nationally. We learn in school when we have a compelling reason to learn.

BUILDING ON STRENGTHS

Because high schools favor quiet approaches to learning and thinking, we lose a good number of students who learn actively, visually, reflectively, or socially—interacting with other people. When a class insists on students learning within a particular mode, student who use their minds in other ways begin to fail. Whatever their strengths might be, they are forced to begin learning on a foundation of weakness, then work to remove apparent deficits. Dreary work. When they try to learn by attacking deficiencies, their abilities, interests, and aspirations cannot feed energy to the tasks they face. Personalized learning begins with the unique strengths a student brings to school, then helps the student extend and elaborate on those strengths. Fortified by success, a student can begin working on other areas by adapting existing skills and knowledge to take on new tasks.

Chris struggled through his first two years of high school. Clearly bright, highly energetic, and unquestionably charming, he had a constellation of talents that found no fitting place in most formal classes, except for mathematics, in which he was strong. In other classes, his attention shifted too fast for the tasks he was required to complete. You can see in his interview how an initial focus on failure slowly gave way to the recognition of intellectual abilities.

Chris (11th Grade)

I was supposed to be in Pathways first semester, but I was one of the very few who did not get in. I was really upset, angry that I had to go through another semester of regular school—and I did badly, again. I really wanted to get in. I need 13 credits before this semester ends. I want to graduate. If I do things really well, I could be almost on track. I reapplied with passion to get in. If I wasn't accepted, I would drop out.

Demands make me not want to do anything. When I jump right into the middle of work, it's just overwhelming, so I get frustrated and I quit. I was not too good at doing homework. Oh God, this is what I have to do and it sucks. Like reading: I can't read unless there is a book that just embraces me. I have a really short attention span. I have ADHD [attention deficit hyperactivity disorder]. I can't do the homework at home.

I am a very odd-working creature; I just get distracted. The way I process things is different. I don't think the same about a lot of things. My mind won't let me do it. I get angry. Frustrated. I have not invested, but I notice and accept my flaws, and see what I am doing wrong. Even when we are being self-directed, there are things we have to do. There is a big open path, and then there are certain parts that narrow right down.

I know random facts. I can spell antidisestablishmentarianism in 3 seconds. Random facts. I can tell you that tropical fish can survive in blood. I get math. I am in pre-calc. I look at any algebra problem and I can see it. I would like to take another algebra course. When I think about something hard, I can see it. When I make an argument, it's thought out. I think about it really hard and really fast. I present it with force. I really like to talk with people online. I like to talk with them. I have friends from all over the place. From California, Oregon, Tennessee, Texas, Florida, North Carolina, South Carolina, all over the place. A fourth of the states.

Things that grab my attention stay there. Once I learn something, it sticks. A little reminder will hit me, wham, it's right there. I played in *Guitar Hero* tournaments, and I came in first twice, and I came in third twice. I won $200, a T-shirt, a poster, and a guitar—a real guitar. Video games are my God-given talent. In *Call of Duty* [a computer game], there are different maps; I walk myself through the map, different houses and rooms, and I can see it in that form. I can remember the whole thing. I also have a wide attention span. I can sometimes listen to three people at once. I can think myself back and pick up and hear what they said. My mind moves fast.

When Chris graduated, he had not designed his Pathway toward mathematics or video games. Instead, he slowly had begun working with other students on their Pathways projects. He liked learning that way. Then, he made several visits to rehabilitation settings with his girlfriend. They brought companion dogs to visit old people in a nursing home and volunteered at community events. In his second year, he became a Pathways leader, helping manage the Space, running discussions with new students, teaching computer game structure, and, finally, team-teaching with Principal Andy Kepes and Caroline Camara and Maureen Deppmann in the Middle School Pathways Exploratory course. In ways that may have surprised even him, Chris began his path with video games, experienced pride in his ability to visualize math, and discovered that he enjoyed working with others.

His talents and interpersonal skills fit perfectly and expanded rapidly—into teaching, where multitasking at high speed may not be a great disadvantage. He had reassembled established strengths to fashion new strengths that would let him move even further. Consulting with newer students, conducting seminars, and working with the Pathways staff, he moved smoothly to graduation, but chose to remain at Pathways for another semester to work with Pathways kids.

Artificial Challenges

Posing artificial challenges that high school aged people do not recognize as important cannot provoke focused inquiry. Most classroom tasks may challenge the intellect but fail to spark personal commitment or interest. They focus immediately on objective "other" without engaging the subjective "self":

- Compare and contrast the French and American revolutions.
- Explain how green algae affect a wetland ecosystem.
- A boat leaves Nashville at 1:00 p.m. while another boat leaves New Orleans at . . .
- Write a letter of congratulations from Vergil to Julius Caesar.

Artificial tasks might inspire a few students but certainly not the majority sitting through 5 or 6 hours of classes.

Sitting in classes but failing a test is punishing. How would it feel to enter classroom knowing that a test is waiting— and that you will not do well? For 10 to 12 years, you have never done well. You have taken many tests, looked at the red number at the top of the page, and seen that you did not succeed—again. You got things wrong. Something was missing. You did not understand what was being asked. Perhaps the best grade you have received is one of those Cs that teachers reserve for the kids who regularly show up in class, but never excel and rarely complain. You looked to the left and right, and saw that some people did excel. They always excelled. What's different about them? Gradually, foreknowledge that you have already failed helps reduce your anxiety as well as effort. With nothing to gain, you have nothing to lose. Your defensive passivity and resignation deepen over the years. You disengage.

From a string of failures, most of us learn to try something else or just to lower our expectations. From a year or two of school failure, you might conclude that you do not have what it takes to make good in school. You are dumb. School must be designed for somebody else—such as those well-dressed kids at the front of the room. You have learned to sit in the back. You do not try to complete assignments any more. What's the use? You have learned most profoundly that effort will not pay off. In fact, working hard and then failing anyway is worse than just failing. Being forced into a chair to experience another painful failure makes you resentful and angry with both teachers and successful students. They have a purpose to fulfill while you are just being compelled by law and convention to waste your time. You feel no purpose in trying fecklessly to meet a meaningless challenge.

Too many students arrive at high school having already concluded that their personal hopes, talents, and aspirations find no connection to their class schedules, within which they must spend 6 hours a day for 4 years. In high school, most learning falls squarely into abstract disciplinary categories: mathematics, English, science, social studies, and maybe a language, with a few electives, which then fall into discrete blocks in a uniform schedule. But high school students often prefer "real" challenges to playing with abstract ideas. Many high school students—perhaps all—want a chance to try themselves against specific and even physical challenges that ignite their energy and dreams, promising to earn them recognition. Most students have developed strengths based on personal interests and experience, often outside of school, so personalized learning has to occur "one kid at a time," extending unique skills and aspirations toward increasingly complex challenges.

Meaningful Challenges

Most high school students respond energetically to challenges that prove they are moving toward autonomy and respect in the eyes of adults and peers. A driver's license, house sitting, going away on a weekend, and getting a job for pay provide them with incontrovertible evidence that the privileges of adulthood may soon come within their grasp. High school rarely gives them a similar way to see themselves moving toward independence. Far more challenging than grades are tasks of the outside world, mainly those carried out by adults. Engaging students in learning begins with identifying the challenges in adult roles to which they will respond with energy and curiosity, in farming, art, education, child-rearing, or construction, for example. Authentic challenge cannot be assigned; it has to be discovered through experience and clarified over time through dialogue with advisors and adult mentors.

Even before the beginning of Pathways, Mount Abraham students began stringing together a year or two of independent studies to complete large personal projects, some of a magnitude that startled the school community into wondering how many more students would want to take on a serious challenge. Before Pathways, one student designed, built, and flew a full-scale version of a 1937 biplane, crashing it twice before safely enrolling in engineering school. Another looked at a devastated floodplain by the river, then designed and helped build a town park on the ravaged site. Two designed and built a rotating sound stage for the auditorium. Beginning in a ninth-grade earth science course, two Mount Abraham girls spent three years assembling course projects and independent studies to develop the wood chip generator that now heats the high school. They read the texts, talked to engineers and heating specialists, did a feasibility study, launched a proposal to the school board, and held the silver shovels at the ground-breaking ceremony. Wood smoke rises from the stack that towers over the high school, a testament to audacious inquiry.

Early productions such as these resemble problem solving in the adult world more than they resemble student projects with predetermined products. Authentic problems are no different from the situations adults confront in trying to use knowledge to make a difference in their lives and the lives of others. Such problems are complex and confusing—or they would have been solved already by someone else. They require research into many disciplines and professions, applied with careful thinking as well as trial and error. Incremental progress toward ill-defined goals drives back the limits of what we see as possible.

People respond to a challenge only if they have decided meeting the challenge increases their satisfaction and improves their prospects. They have to believe that they have a chance to make a difference and feel prepared to succeed by prior learning and earlier success. They have set a purpose for themselves that depends on doing well. Most important, high school students have to be absorbed in doing the work itself, the action of taking on a challenge—doing it. Through their work, they begin to imagine a future in which school success makes a difference. They want recognition for their accomplishments. When school learning blocks the path toward such rewards, they lose confidence in their purpose and their ability to achieve success.

When students take on real challenges, their inquiry can change direction rapidly as their growing knowledge changes the shape of what they want to do. One of the original Pathways students set out to write stories and screenplays, but progress in those areas pushed her far beyond them—and she found herself designing computer games. Pressed forward by the evolution of her interests, she took on the challenge of learning math and programming and surprised herself with the progress she made. Her exhibition of the computer games she had designed inspired several others to think about programming games. As a graduate, she now designs Web pages for people across the county.

DESIGNING PATHWAYS BY INCREASING CHALLENGE

At Pathways, inquiry seldom unfolds in a linear pattern. At the beginning, a few ideas arise but fail to catch fire. Then, with the guidance of an advisor, a range of interests widens and expands the scope of exploration. Identification of an interest powerful enough to drive deep inquiry can take weeks, months, or the whole year. Little of this initial work can be done through books. Purpose usually evolves through experience, some of it dull and discouraging, but other experiences more engaging, leading toward new areas of inquiry. Making a film, raising hogs, volunteering at a hospital lab, or rebuilding an engine engages a student or not. When students settle on a challenge, more effort becomes available for further kinds of inquiry and increased willingness to take on complex problems. When students begin narrowing their focus, advisors feel freer to interject bigger challenges, more reading and writing, and more detailed information gathering. A study of Canada geese, for example, might start with the desire to hunt them before school every morning, but soon take flight into goose nutrition, seasonal eating variations, plant physiology, weather patterns, and goose aeronautics. So went one Pathways 10th-grade semester. An authentic challenge does not stand still while a student works out easy answers. Fraught with complexities, real or authentic challenges expand and grow increasingly engaging as inquiry yields information—revealing further areas of challenge. Advisors work purposefully to stretch inquiry.

PERSONALIZATION AND STUDENT ACHIEVEMENT

Standards-based testing saturates discussions of high school redesign, but few modifications to the high school curriculum actually use test scores to fit instruction to individual needs. Most public discussion focuses on the performance of groups, rather than individuals, featuring comparative scores, levels of proficiency, failing schools, and other terms that convey the idea that institutions, rather than people, are responsible for learning. What if we returned to the older idea that learning is an act of each learner? What if we made room for learning all the knowledge, skills, and abilities that make our society adaptive to change? If test scores teach us nothing else, they show that student performance in high school ranges across an enormous span. Some students score well; others score poorly—and the profile of "answers" for any student shows that each student has learned different things from the same classroom experience. When we decide that all students should meet the same standards in the same way on the same schedule and in the same setting, we overlook the obvious point that the people who fill high school classrooms are unique. In treating young people the same way, we guarantee our failure—and theirs.

Since the publication of *A Nation at Risk* in 1983, efforts at high school reform have largely reinforced the same conception of high school learning that reform was meant to replace. Students are organized into groups that can be taught the same way with the same texts. Students pursue a few prescribed course sequences toward graduation. All students follow the same daily pattern, governed by common rules and a master schedule. Students are graded on the same scale, making it possible to identify a "class rank" for each and award only a few for their accomplishment. Then, on standardized or standards-based tests, students demonstrate their achievement in a narrowly limited number of academic disciplines: English, math, social studies, and science—and their scores range across the scales.

But all learning is personal. High school learning could not produce such a broad range of different results, whether measured on standardized tests or creative projects, if learning were not distinctive in each of us. Learning is active. Learning is effortful. Learning is idiosyncratic to the individual learner. Learning follows personal engagement.

If we cannot engage kids, then we will not see much learning. To redesign the high school experience, we need to base our reform efforts on increasingly complex ideas about how young adults learn, how individuals learn differently, and how to strengthen their ability to ask questions and develop answers for themselves—in active settings where any adult would have to learn in order to succeed.

The sparse research available on personalized settings allows for the possibility that personalization and accountability are not necessarily antagonistic. We might expect that high schools moving to a personalized framework would suffer great declines in the test scores often used to measure academic "rigor," but small size, personalization, and flexibility do not necessarily wreak havoc on accountability. When New York City replaced Julia Richmond High School, a large comprehensive high school of 3,000 students, with six smaller, student-centered learning communities in the Coalition Campus School Project, test scores and other measures of success went up rather than down.

	Student Outcomes: Julia Richmond High School CCSP Average	
	Large Comprehensive	Smaller Student Centered
1995–1996		
Average daily attendance	72%	86.2%
Incident rates (disciplinary)	3.3	1.2
One-year dropout rates	6.1	1.2
Students with reading gains	52.4%	56.9%
11th-grade passing regents exams:		
in reading	79%	80%

(Continued)

(Continued)

	Student Outcomes: Julia Richmond High School CCSP Average	
	Large Comprehensive	Smaller Student Centered
in mathematics	57.5%	76.6%
in writing	75.2%	71.4%
Limited English proficient students with adequate language gains	53%	91.2%

When Boston studied academic success at the smaller, more personalized pilot schools, students in the pilot schools scored higher than students in more conventional schools on the Massachusetts Comprehensive Assessment System (MCAS) standards-based test—84 percent compared with 58 percent. On the mathematics portion, at the 10th-grade level, 80 percent of the pilot students passed while 59 percent passed in other Boston Public Schools (BPS). Tenth-grade math MCAS scores were similarly higher than those posted by BPS high schools. Eighty percent of the students passed the 10th-grade math MCAS test, compared with 59 percent in other city schools. Scores rose in both areas in personalized schools during the high school years. Pilot school students dropped out of high school at lower rates and went to college at higher rates. Adrian Steinberg (2002) noticed the same patterns when she interviewed the graduates of the Metropolitan Career and Technical Center (Met) in Providence, Rhode Island. By their account and in her assessment, all of them graduated at the top of their class—43 valedictorians. Perhaps we have been victims of a false dichotomy in the battle over accountability.

Public schools have to tolerate compromise, generating an acceptable balance among competing priorities. Especially with emergence of smaller schools, differentiated instruction, charter schools, magnet schools, private academies, and home school-ing, secondary education is experimenting vigorously to mix components so each student achieves a level of acceptable pro-ficiency; however, so far, we have relied on setting up separate institutions for different kinds of learning as if school structure, rather than personal effort, generates success. Personalized pro-grams such as Pathways are unique because they are seeking to respond to an enormous variety of personal orientations within a single building holding all the kids. Two basic principles can help balance academic rigor and self-direction:

- Hold all students, teachers, parents, and community members accountable for building *competency in a few essential skills, K–12.* ("Less is more," Theodore Sizer insisted as he developed the Coalition of Essential Schools).
- Encourage students, parents, teachers, and community members to arrange *a wide spectrum of choices* that allow each student to fulfill personal goals.

Under this conception of balance, schools are responsible for ensuring the mastery of essential intellectual and social skills through access to the widest array possible of applied and theoretical knowledge, surrounded by support. Students remain responsible for directing their own learning.

ACCEPTING AMBIGUITY

To develop both the accountability and responsiveness we seek, we will have to accept that our answers change dra-matically as we move from one puzzling situation to the next. We get the most useful answers when we understand that answers emerge incrementally and grow toward coherence slowly. The highest quality of learning grows through com-mitted engagement with intractable problems, the discovery of things that work, and the discovery of truths that actually matter. In the name of social priorities, pressure-driven into the high school curriculum, we have been forcing kids to pursue narrow questions they have not asked, and the results of force-feeding do not necessarily add up to growth.

Like the students themselves, high schools do not improve through a process of linear growth, from pale beginnings toward a bright future. Learning does not lift off the ground the way a Boeing 747 lifts off the tarmac, heading for the bright blue. Learning, on a broad scale or in the individual mind, improves in wobbly cycles. The cycles are infuriating. Personalized learning should aim to reconcile the focus on knowledge and the focus on students, who can learn to gather information from many disciplines as they also practice managing the work of their minds. Aspirations, skills, and knowledge must evolve in connection with each other. Even in itself, accepting ambiguity in working to meet emerging challenges that matter is not a trivial accomplishment.

NAGGING QUESTIONS ABOUT PERSONAL ENGAGEMENT

1. What are the risks that could accompany school personalization?

2. How can we plan to increase engagement among students who may not want to take responsibility for their own learning?

3. As Larry Cuban (2012) has explained, standardization and customized or personalized learning have been competing for public favor for more than 100 years. What factors might lead to the integration of personalization this time? What factors might support the status quo?

2

Patterns of Growth

OVERVIEW

Personalized learning is based on perceptions of how young adults learn, rather than what they learn; personalized learning can provide an organizing structure for whole-school *transformation.* Although discipline-based curricula divide learning into subjects, personalized learning must begin with a coherent set of ideas about how young adults learn to manage their own lives and improve the lives of others. This chapter focuses on six patterns of growth that are noticeable among students who are learning to be independent learners. To avoid implying that these patterns occur separately from each other, I asked students to tell me their stories about their experience in Pathways—in all their complexity—but I did edit the interviews to improve coherence and feature one of the six patterns, without losing their "voices" by oversimplifying, decontextualizing, or depersonalizing their unique perspectives.

PERSONALIZED LEARNING AT MOUNT ABRAHAM

On the Vermont side of Lake Champlain, the Green Mountains slice the state into neat valleys, each with its river and river towns, usually organized into union school districts with one high school and several feeder elementary schools. Mount Abraham in Bristol serves the Five Towns of the Addison Northeast Supervisory Union (ANESU). Bristol is the only town with a stoplight or police department in the school district. In a small place such as Bristol, education is much more personal than political—and change occurs through the interactions of people who come to know each other well. Personalized learning has become a centerpiece of the change process at Mount Abraham, partly because parents and the larger community see learning and teaching as intensely personal, and they have repeatedly observed remarkable demonstrations of achievement by young people among the Five Towns.

From the front door of Mount Abraham you can see through the gap between the rocky crag called Deerleap and the rugged slope of Bristol Cliff all the way to Stark Mountain, home to Sugarbush and Mad River ski areas. From the back of the school, at the edge of an abandoned quarry, you can look across miles of cornfields past mist-shrouded Lake Champlain to the blue Adirondacks. Farm trucks wind their way up the steep hill that becomes Main Street, with its middle-sized grocery store and single block of small shops. From the front entrance, you can watch towering logging trucks rumble down the road from the high forests to drop their loads of hardwood at one of the town's two remaining lumber mills. The school district is now the largest local employer by far.

As "Gateway to the Green Mountains," Bristol has few indigenous industries. Many of its dairy farms have turned into fields of brush and milkweed. The furniture factories are gone. Like Vermont itself, Bristol is relatively poor. Approximately 40 percent of Mount Abe students qualify for free or reduced-price lunch, proportions reflected in Pathways enrollment. People in the Five Towns of ANESU have more opportunities to interact with each other personally than residents of more urban settings, working together on sports programs, cultural activities, and social issues in the region. Growing a new kind of high school in this district has to be a community project. Like other Vermont towns, Bristol can experiment with educational change, if only because it is small and isolated—and nobody from the outside is paying that much attention.

In this small, rural middle/high school of 840, Grades 7–12, approximately 200 (30 percent) of 650 students in Grades 9–12 have undertaken at least one personalized credit in the 2012–2013 school year. In addition, virtually all of approximately 160 students in the middle school take one or two middle school exploratory courses, one initiating student personal learning plans (PLPs) and the other introducing the Pathways Inquiry Process. For any student, the Personalized Learning Department offers credit for independent studies, community service experiences, virtual courses, college courses, and career explorations—sometimes linked to programs at the county vocational and technical center. Conventional courses in civics, biology, physics, history, English, and physical education in the high school have adopted aspects of personalized or project-based learning. Within the Personalized Learning Department, Pathways allows any Mount Abraham student to design a personal pathway to graduation "full time," pursuing personal interests while meeting graduation competencies. Between 35 and 50 Pathways students are full time in Pathways in a semester. Because the program called Pathways helped create the foundation for the Personalized Learning Department and because full-time Pathways students use most of the available options to design their own curriculum, I have used Pathways students as the source of the examples in this book.

PATTERNS OF GROWTH IN PERSONALIZED LEARNING

To make learning personal and active, we have to design an enriched, supporting environment that reinforces an individual's willingness to conduct independent inquiry and ability to succeed. In my interviews of Pathways students, the character of relationship between individual student drives and a supportive school culture seemed to follow a natural growth pattern, from an inner core of drives that can be strengthened to an outer ring of challenge and opportunity where students need support. Thinking about support for personalized learning may be easier to see if we represent internal drives and needed support as a flower with six petals. With the student at the center, internal drives push out toward an outer ring of experience, where learning requires support from adults.

To engage students in learning, we can think about incubating growth from the inside out, accentuating natural

Figure 2.1   Areas of Growth in a Personalized High School Experience

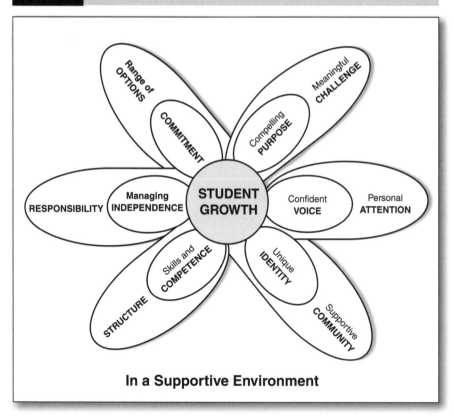

In a Supportive Environment

drives among young adults while arranging rich and expansive support for personalized inquiry, such as books, computers, travel, project materials, peer coaches, job opportunities, internships, advisors—and caring adults, whether teachers or community members who have developed a career in a student's field of interest. Technology expands the world of accessible information, through websites, chat groups, and blogs, for example, while also increasing the number of media students can use to show what they have learned, such as prezis, word processors, video editors, and animation and graphic software. In my interviews with Pathways students, I saw that the majority of students grew active in all six areas illustrated by the image of the flower, but each student grew most vigorously in one or two. The stories that follow illustrate those six patterns of growth, appearing in the unique experience of each student, with some reference to necessary support from the surrounding community of students and adults.

1. Growing a Purpose

When students face meaningful *challenges related to their interests*, they begin to develop and clarify a *purpose* for learning.

Most high school students have not had a great deal of opportunity to figure out the lives they want to lead. In personalized learning, the first step is to help students understand a compelling purpose for their work. That purpose is usually embedded in earlier challenges at which they have succeeded with enough joy to want further success. For some, raising an animal brings the joy of success. For others, printmaking, automobile design, basketball, family life, or fishing ignites some purpose. Facing early blossoming, an advisor works to identify challenges that will inspire a student to expend energy on learning—the way they do when facing an authentic challenge outside of school.

For some, such as Ashley, sitting in a classroom room without accepting a purpose for sitting was agony.

Ashley (12th Grade)

I sat there, and sat there and stayed there through classes— not learning. . . . In one ear and out the other. I would be learning more not in school than in school. I would not be learning about the real world. It was really frustrating. I was really sick of school. I would have flunked out. I was not learning anything. I nearly dropped out to earn my GED. You are locked up. In normal school, they tell you what to do.

I heard about Pathways from my friends, and it was kind of my only choice by that time. I decided that school at Mt. Abe was not working. I was excited. Now, at Pathways, we get to see the working world. In school, you don't get to see real stuff.

First, I did a project on mental health. Then soap-making. I still work on making soap a little, but basically my main project is teaching snowboarding. I got a full-time job at Sugarbush last winter. Every other day, I would drive myself over the Appalachian Gap. I learned a lot about winter driving, getting there on time and job skills. Originally, I wanted to just teach snowboarding, but then it branched out to all of the components of snowboarding. I feel I am going to use this stuff later, as opposed to . . . history. I could have continued doing my first project on mental illness. When I started snowboard-ing, I liked it. That really got me amped up. I applied for a teaching job. I was competing with college kids. I got the job.

I have learned a lot. I learned the proper way to teach snowboarding. The other day, I recorded myself waxing a snowboard, and then I uploaded it to the computer, edited it, and now it's a good little film. I made some little "prezis"—fun little animations. I am thinking about making a snowboard. I did all the online research, for my prezi. Things that I heard from people. I used all that for my first presentations.

Then, I learned how to teach little kids. To talk to them. Talking to little kids, teaching them how to snowboard. Every kid is different. There was one girl—she ended up breaking her wrist at the end of the lesson. She was definitely not a snowboarder. She was really scared. But she ended up doing awesome. I have videos of it, even though she clearly didn't know much at the beginning. I will show the video at my exhibition.

I taught Russell [her advisor] to snowboard. That would not happen at regular school. Up there on the mountain, he was really good. Usually, people just improve one level at a time: red, yellow, green, blue, black. Black is the highest. He got to green in one day. Normally that would take three or four days.

Luckily, Pathways was there. Pathways is like preparing you for the real world. You are learning about things you will take with you, for later. Clearly, if it's something you want to learn, you are passionate about, you can learn. Now at Pathways, I'll sit down and get on my computer, and I usually have a little "to-do list" of stuff that I am working on. Basically, I decide where I am going to start. I do bits and pieces, and eventually they will all come together. I decide what I am doing. I start working. I wander away, then shift to something else for a while.

I feel I can use this stuff next year at Nevada College or Rocky Mountain College. I am sure I am going to use this stuff. I plan to go to college for recreation management. This summer I am going to take a college class at the Community College, Introduction to College Studies. I will get a free tuition voucher. In college you are on your own. At Pathways you are on your own. I can sit down myself and number out all the things I have to do—and do them.

In her senior year, with two other Pathways students, Ashley began designing and building a snowboard park for the high school, while still planning to study recreation management when she went to college in Colorado the next fall.

2. Growing Identity

Within a supportive *community*, students can build a sense of *distinctive identity* based on recognizable achievements.

Students coming into a high school from a sixth- or eighth-grade classroom immediately encounter a school culture much larger and more impersonal than anything they have previously experienced. They quickly gravitate to smaller cultures where they can fashion some kind of identity, often based on similarities rather than differences. Cliques abound: jocks, nerds, cheerleaders. . . . Afterschool clubs and teams can provide an anchor for some, but many others drift off to groups that have no association with a school, including both church groups and street gangs. I have asked many students what group they belong to. None have said that they are preps or Goths. They think of other kids as preps and Goths. Without recognition for unique talents, interests, and aspirations, they still want to feel unique unto themselves. Despite their propensity to bunch up, high school students crave recognition for personal qualities.

Miles worked closely with Russell over a year of frustration. Clearly, Miles had a bright and active mind, but he was not using it purposefully at the high school:

Miles (12th Grade)

I was failing most of my classes. Everything I was doing was waste. I wanted to spend my time at school doing something worthwhile. Like right now, I could be working full time. I am a perfectly able-bodied young man. I could spend some time stocking shelves at Shaw's, as long as I moved up from there. That's what everybody else does. Even when you go to college, you end up waitressing. That's nothing I can't do. It's all these hours. School is stressful. When I was a little kid I wondered why I didn't get paid for going to school. It's stressful, like if I don't do well I will ruin the rest of my life, the guidance counselors say. That's their opinion.

My first project was self-sustainability. I was really interested in living in the woods, but then I saw it was not sustainable. It's not something I can actually do. So I wanted to direct my path toward something useful. I really didn't do much. I played around on Craigslist, I read my books, did a lot of things that are not Pathways work. When it came to exhibitions, I felt I had done so much less than others. But I did a lot of thinking.

I sugared a bunch that spring. I learned what it was like to stay up all night boiling and sterilizing stuff. I was doing poetry for like hobby fun stuff. Poetry is just self-expression. It was not necessarily work I did for Pathways. And maple trees? I just wanted to make sugar out of my own interest. Poetry got me a little credit.

Now, I can say what it's like to do yard work. I can say what it's like to fry foods at Wocky's restaurant at $9 an hour. It's three nights, 4:30 to 10:00. That's 15 hours—plenty—$150 for working half a week. I realize what it's like to come hope super tired, after going to school for 6 hours, then working for 3 or 4 hours. It was frustrating and stressing.

I just finished my work in Lifetime Math, which I really like because it teaches math skills, like buying cars. It coincides with my life skills project, where I am practicing living skills, getting a job. Then next I have this course for my firefighting license—four blocks, four times a week, both semesters. By the end of that, I will be able to take the firefighter test.

I am turning toward wilderness medicine because I am really interested in helping people, something I wouldn't mind doing for a living while I sustain my personal survival. I finished the wilderness first-responder rescue course. I have a card, a really nice thing to have. I really hadn't worked Pathways until the First Responder class, kind of a foot in the door. I am taking a community college course over the summer called Introduction to College Studies. After that, I can sign up for another free college course at the community college for more college credit, that I can also transfer to high school credits, then firefighters training and wilderness rescue certification. Then during the spring, I stuck with this program.

Miles passed both the introduction to college and a medical terminology course at the community college in his senior year at Mount Abraham, graduated with his class, and began looking at emergency medicine as a college concentration.

His final reflection essay before graduation describes the essence of the identity he developed over three years:

I have changed as a person in the sense that my priorities have gone from hanging outside and doing what makes me happy by impulse—to finding and pursuing a passion, gaining accreditation, and establishing myself as a member of the larger community.

3. Gaining Personal Voice

To develop, express, and test a *personal voice*, students need *focused attention* from caring adults.

I sat down to interview Logan in his second year of work at Pathways. He had been a successful student in his early classes in the high school, but his grades began to drop in ninth grade. While rejecting the demands of conventional classes, he remained largely unaware of what he might be able to do without a conventional structure and schedule. At Pathways, he "shopped" for a semester, then began to focus. With a growing interest in student engagement, he attended an education conference in New Hampshire with teachers and administrators from Mount Abe and twelve other schools, surprising himself by taking a prominent role in the discussions and gaining confidence in his voice. As the conference broke up, he found he had earned the respect of adults and young people—and began to develop some commitment to alternative educational practices. Now, he is writing a history of high school practices and planning for his own conference on student engagement.

Logan (11th Grade)

> It took a while to find what I wanted to do. I started off with small business management because I thought business management would give me a really good set of skills, no matter what I wanted to do. I didn't want to work for someone else, a boss who would say do this or that. But then I figured out that I didn't have much interest in business and lost motivation, and it took me a little while to figure out another interest and pursue the options for that. I tried to shoot off into other projects.
>
> I attended a conference with teachers over the summer that showed me how much interest there was in alternative learning, how many different possibilities there are. The teachers invited me and Miles to come along to get some school credit. We both had low expectations for the conference, but it did turn out to be really interesting. I saw that working together could be a quick-flowing process, with movement through you and the teachers, with teachers that worked well together. We had a lot of opportunities to express our views about Pathways and how the school structure was shaped.
>
> Probably the coolest thing was that we had a student panel. Four of us went up before the entire collection of students, teachers, principals, and officials. We were talking

about the integration of technology. Technology is something most kids my age understand well. Teachers had biases because they have seen it used improperly. So it was cool to be able to talk to them about the uses of technology, and we could see how it could be used so we could talk to them about uses with technology that they had not thought possible. We talked about Facebook and how networking tools were not being used. It was really helpful for me because sometimes I get stuck with my words. When I have prodding from students and teachers, I have to make a flow and make connections. It stimulated my mind.

I feel like the flow in my head is pretty streamlined when I am working with an adult and I can get feedback and improve my work. I did see a lot of "wow" and lots of "thanks-yous" and "congratulations," and I felt a strong sense of accomplishment. I was proud of being able to present ideas to people who had gone through a lot of education, people who had worked in the field for 30 years.

Back at Mount Abe, I started out trying to figure out how to create a really engaging atmosphere because that was a problem in Pathways. It's hard for kids to move from one kind of learning to another, without some kind of structure to guide them through all the obstacles. So I was going to try to find a way to get them more interested and show them the potential that I saw in this program. I came up with an oral communication project because I saw that when kids were talking about their projects, they were much more interested. They did not like to write because it could block the flow of creativity, if they were not good writers. There was a lot of interest, and it worked pretty well.

Coming back to Mount Abe, I felt I had found an interest that was a great outlet for my creative skills, and it was something that would help other people, a big piece of why I was there. Then, I had to come up with ideas and bounce them off Josie and Ms. Camara and yourself and others. I could address the problems in public education and start to solve them through alternative learning. I identified other groups that are really interested, and I identified problem areas and the benefits of alternative education. I feel recognized for my work here.

One thing that comes up a lot is creativity and how important it is to foster it in order to cope with the way the world is changing. The idea is that we are still teaching the same kind of problems as in the industrial age. That's not the kind or worker we need now. We need innovators. We need an innovative citizen.

Logan conducted seminars with Mount Abe students, sat on the Pathways design team, and monitored the Pathways space when the advisors need to talk with each other. As he developed his personal voice, he became a leader.

4. Earning Respect

In learning how to manage their freedom, *students* need defined *responsibilities* so they can earn *respect for their accomplishments.*

Despite the myth that young adults would prefer to be idle, they most want to be absorbed, seeking progress, satisfaction, and engagement. Students revel in their freedom, but begin to feel uncomfortable when they see that they are not using it well, when they see the respect they earn simply by actively assuming responsibility for an important job. After a semester learning how to use Pathways, John discovered freedom in his passion for fire and rescue.

John (12th Grade)

Before Pathways, school was a huge struggle for me. I would do my best and always get behind, and at the end of the semester or quarter, I would spend a week trying to do the work and catch up to pass the class. When I got in here, it really clicked. I got everything together and started busting out. This year has been an awesome year. I guess I have done about four years of high school in one year in Pathways.

It took a couple of weeks to get used to Pathways. I talked with Gerrie about joining the Rescue Squad and Fire Department. I never had time for it because of school. She called the station, and they said I was old enough and eligible to apply, so she says, "Let's drive down there right now." In school, it would be planning for next week. But she said, "Let's do it right now." We are doing it right now, and we are just going to do it." I applied for the Firefighter Course. I got all these connections started and from there took on all of them at once, writing stuff down, going to classes, running shifts—working hard.

This semester I am doing firefighting and rescue. I am doing rescue at Vergennes Area Rescue squad, pulling 12-hour shifts. Every Wednesday night, I have training with the Monkton Fire Department. Every Thursday, I have training with Rescue. Halfway through this semester, I graduated from Firefighter I, the 210-hour Essentials Course for firefighting. Boy, that was a hard course. The reading level! The book breaks down into sections, like Hazardous Materials and Fire Science, the different consistencies of wood and BTUs. I spent 4 hours every Thursday night at the course, with weekly exams and practicals. Once I got into it, running calls, my passion for rescue became more powerful than fire.

You read the chapters. The weekly tests were hard. If you failed, you had two more tries. You had to get 80 percent to pass. If you fail then, you have to do the whole program again, after waiting a year. It delays the whole process of graduating. You have to pass everything in order to pass the course. To take the final test and final practical, you have to have all the parts done. Last year, I had to retake two exams. You have to continue taking classes. There are a bunch of refresher courses. Every year you have to earn CEUs to keep your certification. I have already started.

In high school classes, I was not a test taker. I would study and study and have it all in my head, sit down—and have a test in front of me. . . . I had a hard time remembering. I would go to Rescue, and a lot of the guys were also firefighters, about 25 percent were also on Rescue, so I was on duty and I'd say, "Hey, you want to help me study?" And they would quiz me. They had already been through it. It was definitely a big help working with somebody one-on-one, a person I could just talk to. One night, we had a couple of guys from the class who all had dinner and, we all took the test together.

During Rescue calls, I am in the back, dealing with patients, from car accidents or basic calls where someone calls Rescue with a situation. I am the one starting oxygen. I take vital signs, blood pressure. I am not allowed to do IV [intravenous] yet. It goes by certification levels—first responder, the EMTI [emergency medical technician-intermediate], and paramedic. Right now, I am just an EMTA. Once I work myself up, I can do intravenous and blood sugar. I usually assist the crew chief. Like at car accidents, I get in and do patient stabilization and get the patient out and into the ambulance. I am kind of a "go-first." I am in the middle of things.

I have had some tough calls. With a stroke patient, time is of the essence. I had never run with anyone on that crew, but we worked together really well, just a last-minute group put together to run the call. We all pulled together. The doc came out from Fletcher Allen Hospital and said, "Everything was perfect. Your work probably saved him because he didn't know he was having a stroke. Another 20 minutes, he would have been paralyzed." It is very hard to save a cardiac patient; there may be a 90 percent chance that it is too late. If they can't call 911, you get there at a late stage. After a call like that, they have therapist come and talk with us. We have to sit back and say, we have done what we've done. This is what I did. There are hard times. It comes with the territory. I did what I could do.

Once a year, we do a big annual meeting, all the departments in Addison County. There are two big awards. I was awarded Junior Firefighter of the year for Addison County. I also got the award with Rescue as Rookie of the Year. I am doing my anatomy and physiology next year at Vermont Tech. Once I get out of high school, I will go to the Paramedics Programs. From there I might go to Boston or New York and run with the big guys. I will still do volunteer firefighting.

Last semester at exhibitions, I showed all the credits I earned. With Vergennes Rescue, I wrote stories to get an English credit. First semester I did a really big history credit, studying the history of firefighting, how it started, the gear they had, different methods, and how it progressed until now. This semester, I compared the two semesters, the growth I had gained. Going into Pathways, I had horrible organization. I showed how I organized everything and kept things straight. That was the one thing I could never do, keep myself organized.

My final exhibition, I showed my growth over the year, how I started and how I finished. Being on time. But organization was the big one. Being able to sit down and do 3 to 4 hours [of] studying. I could never study before. I could not even do an hour. I always zone off or go distract myself. This year, I can just sit down with a book and get the work done.

5. Growing Commitment

Students need to see a wide range of *authentic choices* through which they can develop increasingly focused *commitment to learning.*

Students cannot commit themselves to a particular pathway unless their high school opens the way for a wide assortment of choices for exploration, with clear processes that help a student take action and follow through. If there are no choices, students cannot build commitment. Although a student's choices may look random at any moment, in retrospect they form an organized pattern that looks a lot like growth.

Niles (12th Grade)

The main reason I chose Pathways is that I was losing interest in the classes, especially English and social studies. I wasn't interested in the topics and doing the work. I wasn't working to my full potential. I probably did best in my sophomore year, but in my junior year, second semester, I saw too much work that was not relevant to what I wanted to be doing. At Pathways, I could focus on the real world and do something I was interested in. Now, I have six periods of credits, including AP English and AP calculus, but I switched out of English. I am interested possibly in an engineering career, so calculus would be more relevant to my career than English.

For my first project, I decided to apply for work at the snow park at Sugarbush Ski Area, where I have been an instructor for three years. I wanted to do snowboard park design, designing the rails and fabricating structures out of steel and wood for jumps and tricks. Gerrie called Sugarbush, and I got a call from the director of the parks crew, and I got a full paid, full-time on the parks design crew, three days a week and vacations. We went down to a building that looked like a culvert where they were working on a fabrication project and I got to look around. They had designed all the rails and [laid] it all out on CAD/CAM in 3D. I have wanted to do this since ninth grade. At the time, Sugarbush was working on its Facebook page, which is how they do scheduling and events. So I started working on the Facebook page.

On the side, I am planning a snowboard park for the school. We went down to Casella's landfill, which they had bulldozed over and planted grass. We got permission from their board of directors, so we went to the town, got a tax map, and checked out zoning. We covered everything we thought would be issues. We walked around the hill with two lawyers.

Meanwhile, I had a couple of rails I had made at home. I found a guy on Craigslist who had a 12-foot-long box of rails and culvert. I had a whole lot of supplies but just need the land. Gerrie is still talking with the lawyers. I think it's great I am in a program like this, from the tax maps and lawyers to engineering, Web graphics and design. It's all real-world experience.

I definitely want to go to college, but because I have been changing my focus from engineering, to architecture to design to graphics, I have applied to colleges in design, engineering, and graphics, including filmmaking.

With several college choices in view, Niles chose to enroll in a local college with majors in all of his areas of interest, but he graduated leaning toward film and graphics.

6. Growing Competence

Students want *success* in their work, but they need *enough structure* to help them build *competence.*

Aidan enrolled in Pathways with the single-minded purpose of drawing characters for an invented land, one mythical character after another. He had been drawing characters for three years, living in in the homeland of the Yeti, surrounded by enemies of many stripes. He had been drawing pictures of characters since he was 14, but he had not written much, nor was he particularly interested in learning to write. His project developed as a way to use his established skills in drawing to create an organizing structure, a plot: from situation to complication to crisis to resolution. Working from his strong interest in drawing toward considerable challenge in writing, he set out to write and illustrate a graphic novel, using his drawings as a basis for writing.

With the support from Frances, his full-time instructional aide, in his IEP Aidan began to map out a series of events around which he could weave a story that would string his pictures together. As the story line spooled out, inspiring even more drawings, an increasingly coherent pattern formed—an organizing plot. Frances supported his evolution throughout his senior year, helping in him create the story line, write text, convert it to printable pages, lay out the novel, enclose it in an elaborate cover, and then move on into electronic media. With guidance and editing from Pathways advisors and Frances, his written language began to match his imaginative drawings, and his text brought the pictures into sequence. As exhibition time approached in December, he began getting ready to publish and present a printed version of *King Yeti*, his first graphic novel, about 15 pages in length.

Aidan first read *King Yeti* to an audience of peers, parents, and other adults at Pathways senior exhibitions in an art gallery on Main Street and was recognized by Pathways students and advisors for making the best presentation. At the Flynn Theater in the City of Burlington, he read his graphic novel and showed slide presentation pages from one shot to another, receiving an award for the best art in the competition. He had experienced the whole process of developing a graphic novel from conception to publication, with a media presentation. He had already received the two awards, but his purpose continued to evolve, and the size of the challenge continued to grow. But after his first book, his purpose continued to evolve.

During his last semester, he wrote more than 25 pages of solid text and drew a portrait gallery for his characters. He explained his next plot to me:

Aidan (12th Grade)

The next one starts off with a boy being found by a river, a homeless young man. Then he joins a crew of pirates. They find an old man on a rock and travel on to the home of corsairs, led by a pirate. It goes back to the Yetis. A lot of adventures happen. The pirates try to fight the Yetis, trying to capture a fort.

Figure 2.1 Page From a Graphic Novel

At about this same time, Prince Elmurph and his villains reached Lamarvalles Forest. They had no idea the Phicaris were going to help the Yetis, but they would find out soon enough.

Elmurph's one brave band of boldest Yaimarie planned to kill the Yetis. Elmurph is their sovereign.

Source: Copyright © Aidan Collins. Used with permission.

Aidan continued his spoken narrative to me for at least 10 minutes, following a strong thread of connected events with several subplots. For Aidan, a Pathways plan became a way to meet the specifics of an individual education plan (IEP), and more, to demonstrate unusual competence in a challenging endeavor.

LEARNING THROUGH RELATIONSHIPS

As students skilled at managing projects grew more numerous, they began to provide support and modeling for beginners. The influence of experienced peers soon affected the tone and quality of work in the Pathways rooms, and Caroline began to formulate specific tasks for the skilled veterans. As Caroline explained it:

> Logan said to us last week when we pulled out for a meeting, "People work so much better when you guys aren't around." When we get out of their way, they do what they are supposed to do. Respect toward that student leader in the room is part of community building.
>
> Chris can run the room. He is stepping up. He is one of them who gets it. He says, "This is what I have to do in order to get out of here." He is coteaching the Pathways course for middle school students with Andy (the principal). He is going to run the class today, and Andy will not be here. We wanted to sign him up for ¼ credit. He said, "No, I want a full credit. What do I have to do to earn a full credit?" Last year he was a minimalist who wanted to know what he had to do to pass. Now, it's "What do I have to do to earn more credit?" We work that out. He says, "Sure, I can do those things."
>
> We were really excited when we came up with this new student leadership team idea. We need somebody to be the supervisor in the room. We were thinking of behavior management. It quickly became learning management. "Logan, how do we do this? How do we do that?" The

older kids were getting really desperate to set up a "culture of learning." Logan has picked up on that. He is getting how this thing works. The culture is changing.

Learning occurs during interactions among students and adults who come to resemble a "learning community" when they recognize that their learning is mutual as well as personal.

Nagging Questions About Student Growth

1. How can a high school support each student's struggle for independence and the community's need for predictable order at the same time?

2. What features should a high school adopt to support growth? What features should it consider dropping or changing?

3. What skills would teacher/advisors need to support individual growth?

3

Shaping the Process of Inquiry

At Pathways, we don't teach students what to think. We teach them how to think.

—Caroline Camara

OVERVIEW

The five Mount Abraham Graduation Competencies give students a clear, steady target for their work each semester while they slowly gather evidence that they are progressing toward higher levels of achievement. The semesters follow a sequence of seven phases that move students from "big" but vague ideas to specific plans in a wide variety of activities, during which they create and gather evidence of learning for their exhibitions and portfolios. Veteran Pathways students often simplify this sequence by following the trajectory of earlier projects toward new challenges. Whatever evidence they accumulate through projects, the process itself is a pattern of learning, and the competencies explain its purpose.

KEEPING THE TARGET STEADY

Guidelines for managing the learning process were not available when the program began; they were developed after the pilot semester revealed that some students could not meet the standards without a clear sense of how they could hit defined targets. Now, students work closely with an advisor to design a personal plan—setting a purpose for their study, developing questions that need answers, and gathering information from a variety of sources. Most test their aspirations through direct experience with an adult in the community who has made a career from interests similar to their own, and students take on new internships when their interests shift. Advisors have found that guidelines for project development increase the sense of freedom students experience, probably because they can see themselves moving toward their purpose within a semester.

Pathways students map pathways toward high school graduation one semester at a time, developing inquiry projects and classes based on their personal interests, strengths, and aspirations, in cycles that incrementally improve the skills they will need to succeed as adults. Most Pathways students take a mathematics class each semester, and most add high school classes, college courses, and virtual courses that fit their evolving plans, but projects are the medium for meeting most graduation standards (see Figure 3.1 Mount Abraham Competency Indicators). In every project, they write a great deal: essays, reflections, stories, annotated bibliographies, progress reviews, letters of inquiry, and responses to the "punch lists" that advisors develop to keep students moving toward proficiency—and they revise their products until they meet competency criteria. They read the equivalent of three books each semester, conduct interviews or observations in the community, and expand their observations into internships. As they go, they build a body of "evidence" for each Mount Abraham Graduation Competency, or standard: communication (reading and writing), critical thinking, independent learning, collaboration, and global citizenship, based on

Figure 3.1 Mount Abraham Competency Indicators

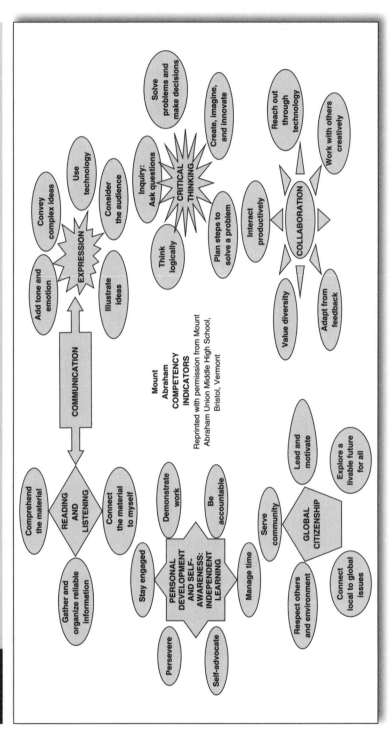

Source: Reprinted with permission from Mount Abraham Union Middle High School, Bristol, Vermont.

21st Century Standards (North Central Regional Educational Laboratory, 2003).

As a semester approaches its close, they develop exhibitions that last an hour. After gathering feedback from audiences and advisors on criteria derived for the Five Competencies, they revise their work so that by the end of a semester, their work is good enough to meet school standards with a B– or better. They display their successful presentations in a cumulative "best-work" portfolio organized by standard. Students design enough credits in classes and projects in a semester to remain in step with classmates toward graduation.

Understanding the importance of planning how to earn credits proved essential to program development. Several times, Pathways advisors called pilot students together to identify and solve problems arising at different phases of the project development process. At the first Council Meeting of Pathways students and adults, advisors posed a central question: What does it take to earn a Pathways credit?

> Chris said: "It really depends on the project. It varies by what you are doing."
>
> Another student replied: "The steps in the process are as important as the product. You should be able to show how you worked with the information so the product makes sense."

Indeed, the early idea of basing credits on specific products and using exhibitions to explain the process of acquiring skill in the competency areas remains central to the organization of semesters at Pathways. Figuring out how many credits a student will earn over a semester occurs in a cycle of adjustment and feedback sometimes lasting the full semester, so each student knows what will be required to qualify for graduation with peers (see Figure 3.2).

The program now introduces rubrics for the graduation competencies throughout the semester to ensure students

Figure 3.2 Proposing Graduation Credits by Developing a Proposal That Describes Products, Steps, Setup Targets, and Criteria

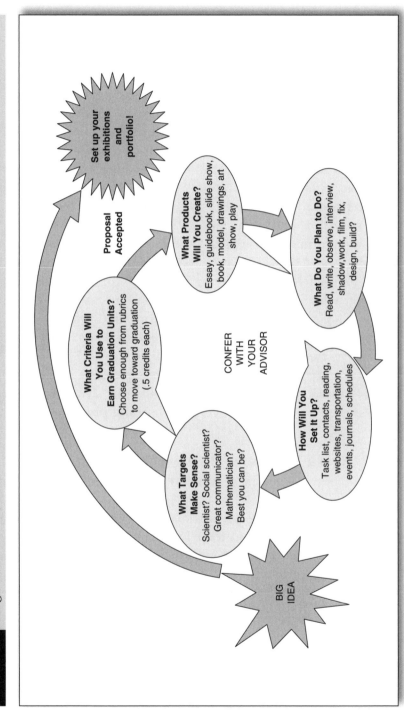

Source: Reprinted with permission from Mount Abraham Union Middle High School, Bristol, Vermont.

regularly connect their work to assessment criteria. They begin each semester by focusing on the rubric for "Independent Learning," giving advisors and veterans a chance to explain what it will take to succeed and work new students into the process. Advising during the first eight weeks supports students as they work on "punch lists" of common products required for all students as well as customized products for each project. By the 10th week, the focus has shifted to preparation for exhibitions, and the final two weeks are devoted to revisions that qualify a student for a grade and credits. Although project planning is now recorded and adjusted within a format, it evolves throughout the semester as the student gains understanding and gets new ideas. From initial probes and study, new ideas emerge for exploration, and new opportunities for reading, writing, and community experience become parts of a plan—generating products for final exhibitions. Pathways is still being designed to help students learn how to manage freedom and make it productive—and the whole school has begun to adapt Pathways strategies as part of school transformation. With variation, the structure of a semester now unfolds in seven overlapping phases.

SEVEN PHASES OF PROJECT DEVELOPMENT IN A SEMESTER

The seven overlapping phases become most visible in the stories students tell about their learning. The following sections explain each phase in project development, in a loose pattern the advisors follow through a semester. For each phase, I have included a story from interviews with Pathways students that illustrates both the tone of a specific phase and overlap that occurs as the phases fall into a "pathway" for each student. The stories also serve a larger purpose, which is to show the unique character of student experiences as they work though a semester. Chapter 4 will describe specific "scaffolding" advisors use to keep their advisees moving toward final exhibitions, portfolios, and credit awards.

Figure 3.3   Seven Phases of Project Development

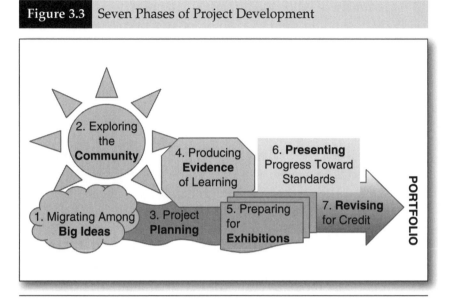

Source: Reprinted with permission from Mount Abraham Union Middle High School, Bristol, Vermont.

Chapter 6 focuses on the mechanics of assessment as it unfolds from a formative stage to final grading.

1. Sifting Through Big Ideas

Beginners in a personalized program often struggle to find that one "big idea" that will bring focus to their work. The first step an advisor takes is to help the student identify personal interests that can be converted to serious inquiry over four months or more. Internet searches, some initial reading, reflective writing, and hours of conversation begin to reveal questions a student wants to answer through research and experience. As Ruby's story shows, however, movement from one idea to the next also occurs through the interaction among students, whose interests may overlap over several semesters, while "big ideas" transform themselves into better ideas. For her first "big idea," Ruby set out to make art, but through four semesters of inquiry, her big idea had migrated toward medicine and brain science. She began with painting, moved to surrealism and history, turned toward mental illness, experimented with soap making, mentored an elementary student—and finished as a senior looking at college in psychology and sociology. In retrospect, she tells a story about confluence, successive approximations that gradually form a big idea strong enough to guide further learning.

Ruby (11th Grade)

First semester, I wanted to do a mentorship and improve my skills in acrylic and oils. With Gerrie, I met with Lynn Root, a science teacher who got awards for surrealism and sculpture. I learned I didn't want to do art. I didn't want other people telling me what to do.

Then, I started making surreal creatures. Chris was going to put them on a computer, but we ended up making actual models with different characteristics. We went online and looked at turtles, cows, ostriches, and lizards and made combinations like turtles + goat + fish. We looked at pictures that let us fit these creatures to their environment. We put it all in the computer and called the creature a "Nacht-demon." Since that name was German, we decided to make the other creatures German, too. The "Nasonkopfzeig" was a wet-headed goat. We had an ostrich/lizard and called it "zerroch-esch." Then I did the drawings.

I talked with Mr. Babbitt, [my faculty mentor in art] about all the materials. After that, we papier-mâchéd the whole thing about five times and added the shell and put on about three more layers. Then, we gave it three white coats with wallpaper plaster. Mrs. Cleary had given us homemade papier-mâché powder. Then, we painted the bright colors, a pink head, a fish with hands, and feathers for the head. The fish had goatlike horns. The body was goat and turtle. The tail was a turtle.

Then, the artists I was studying reminded me of mental illness. Dali took a psychological path from a weird childhood to his art. Ashley and I both had interest in asylums. We liked the buildings—the architecture. But we thought some of the treatments [in the past] were whacked, like lobotomy and electroshock. They still use electroshock in some places. The places were so filled that the patients did not get help. Some were chained to a wall.

Then I got into artistic movements, [and] these names kept coming up. Magritte was in Dadaism, Cubism, and Surrealism. Dali, Magritte, and Braque all knew each other. They all had met Sigmund Freud. That related to my project last semester when I was studying mental illness. For my exhibition, I made a PowerPoint about different artists and their movements.

I also helped Nico with his movie. I was a character and helped him with his script. Jonah, Chris, Conna, Gerald, Charles, and Isaac B. were also actors. Nico, the director, wanted to do a swordfight, so he taught them stage fighting. He duct-taped sticks together. We went to Chris's campground and filmed there. We also had a school setting. Isaac and Nico edited the whole thing on the Apple. He added music and sound effects, cutting scenes, and then we added an ending scene.

I had another project, too, mentoring Patrick Meier, who goes to Bowman School—a sixth grader. He had a helper. He wanted to make an animated film, with clay-mation. We asked about his ideas. A wrecking ball hitting a car in a city. We made the city setting, but then made a UFO [unidentified flying object] out of clay, going across the screen at the top, and it came back to abduct the car. I made a clay person. Peter made a clay alien that went across the screen. We made the props and background. Chris was really good at it, so we used iMovie on a Mac. We made the film, and I showed it at my exhibition. I also helped other people with their projects, Isaac with graphic design, Logan with illustrations for Dante's *Inferno*. I fit all these things together.

I read two books, one on brain science. It seemed to be completely random in its use of science. I didn't agree with it. I liked the book Josie gave me more, *Children With Adult Lives.* The psychologist who wrote it brought the kids with her to different places, even to her own house. Josie's husband works with kids who are schizophrenic or bipolar or retarded. It made me even more interested in psychology. I saw that each person's path is different, based on different experiences.

Now, we are dealing with our punch lists, the bibliography, writing prompts, and exhibition reflections. Next semester, I will be taking sociology and maybe psychology courses. Next year, I want to look at colleges, mostly around clinical psychology. I could become an art therapist or nurse. My sister is a nurse. I want to do an internship at Fletcher Allen Hospital.

Ruby now pursues her interest in psychology at one of the two colleges where she applied.

2. Exploring the Working Community

From questions that emerge during early advising sessions, advisors and students begin to note the kinds of resource material and community experience that might turn into serious inquiry. Most students start by searching the Internet, then struggle with bias and reliability as they try to make information coherent and useful. But the process of exploration is inevitably nonlinear. Meetings fail to happen, people get sick, bright ideas grow pale with exposure—and frustration rises—two steps forward and one step back. Experimentation with freedom creates enormous tension in some students because the process of achieving freedom is not predictable, and satisfaction is not immediate. For most students, experience in the community drives exploration and revision throughout a semester. As they work with their community mentors, students put aside some interests and decide to focus hard on others, as Nick described.

Nick (12th Grade)

I was a mechanic at Junction Auto for about six months. I had my own lift. And I did transmissions and brakes. Putting five cars on a trailer and taking them to the junkyard. Then we all got to work with each other. They got a new tractor, so I learned how to use the tractor and the auto lift. That whole time I was trading my work for truck parts, so I could rebuild my pickup and put an engine in it. It was weird how much trust they put in us. Like why would they give us the keys to a truck and 11,000 pounds of junk metal and send us off?

In the spring, I was at the Russell Farm, where I am now. I was there this morning at 4:30 doing farm chores. We did a lot of sugaring, setting up the buckets and doing a little bit of line work with the vacuum pump. Running the draft horses, big horses.

Breeding animals.

After the chainsaw course I took, I started cutting and skidding logs out, a couple of hundred board feet of forested lumber. I worked on the Christmas tree farm, trimming and limbing, and cutting out all the stumps. There was a lot of blowdown this year, kept me pretty busy. Anybody who knows trees can work all the time. Because of the course, I could step back and size the trees and cutting them the board feet. Life skills! At the Russells' farm I was basically doing chainsaw work and using a skid steer, a little machine with arms. I was using equipment at Junction Auto I used that at the farm.

I did more math in my projects than I would ever have imagined. In welding, being off 1/14 of an inch when you are making something is a lot. With tree cutting, you need to know how diameter relates to area, and you have to use pi, and you have to know 80 percent of diameter. When you are measuring a hinge to get a tree down, 1/32 of an inch counts. You can get a "barber's chair," where the tree splits all the way up. A half inch of lean at the bottom becomes 4 feet at the top of the tree. You can use diameter and length to determine volume of cut limber—with a mathematical equation!

I won the competition day at the Logging Course. I got a 4-foot ruler that lets you get board length without calculation. I have been doing a lot of writing, but not what I was expected to do. I hiked the Long Trail. The entire time I was writing reflections—what I want to do. I could clarify things in my head.

Finally, all these projects began to link together. I was forming a project about mentoring. I was teaching class part of the time, mentoring young adolescents identifying trees, and doing a lot of work with engines and welding. Teaching and fabricating with the kids and also teaching engine repair—how to use the equipment and be safe about it. Kids going up there and welding! Wow!

Nick spent the majority of his Pathways time exploring the local community, where he now works with former mentors from his Pathways experience.

3. Project Planning

Feeling helpless in a conventional classroom, some students grow restless, then resentful—then rebellious. Sterling, who joined Pathways as an eighth grader during the pilot program, had chafed under the regimen of a tight middle school schedule, becoming a regular in the disciplinary room. He has stayed full-time at Pathways since the eighth grade, through internships as a wildlife observer, fishing guide, blacksmith, taxidermist, and inveterate hunter—gradually refining a plan to become a hunting and fishing guide. He has planned and carried out projects on surviving alone in the woods, hunting geese, harvesting lumber, blacksmithing, taxidermy—and, with Russell at the rescue end of the rope, even floating in a freezing pond to understand the process of hypothermia. In successive explorations, he has learned how to plan projects and manage his time getting ready for exhibitions by creating products, writing about them, and developing visuals for his presentations.

Sterling (9th Grade)

Back in regular classes, there is so much going on, you can't really grasp ahold of it. You get homework every night for every class. I am not a big fan of homework. The pace was always heating up. I couldn't keep up with it. In science, as soon as I would understand a topic, I would say, hey, I know how to do this. We would get on to another one. So fast. So fast. At Pathways, I still do a lot of work, but I do it at my pace, and it's more comfortable.

As school goes on and I get into my Pathways routine, I say, OK, I get to do this and that tomorrow. It becomes a lot clearer about what I am going to do. I get my whole week planned out on Monday. I come in with a set plan all ready. I design it, so I enjoy it. In Pathways, I can go home and say I want to be doing this. It makes it a lot easier to work. OK, I made this. This is OK for me to do. I made it, and I want to do it. I actually want to do it.

Pathways is self-designed learning, so you have to know what you want to do before you start on it. A lot of kids say, "Oh, Pathways, that's where you go to can do nothing." Think about it. You go to [regular] school, you get your work, and do it to get your credit. At Pathways, we go to school, we invent our work—and then we have to do it as well to get the credit. At Pathways, you don't get any assignments. You get the guidelines.

In the fall semester, I wrote a couple of stories, five to six pages, then some journal writes and essays. Mostly, I wrote this huge story. I did some research papers and reflections. I did a PowerPoint on guiding, with Bradley Carlston [community mentor] at Champlain Valley Guide Center. Awesome. I did the research on costs, salary, and fees. I want to make money on hunting and fishing. I read this whole book today. And I read the magazine, *Ducks Unlimited*, about conservation, tips for bird calling, updates on species declining while others are booming. There is always a history section, like a decoy found last year that sold for 6 million dollars. The money went to *Ducks Unlimited* for conservation.

The standards have helped along the way. They say, OK, this is what I need to do to earn credit, what I need to get done. I have to follow along on critical thinking. When you do all of those things with one project, you get the credit. Sometimes I didn't know really what I want to do, and how to accomplish it, so I would just look at the posters on the wall or go on Gmail to read about them. Kind of like guidelines to follow.

I am pretty sure I will go to college. If I go to college, I want to try hard to go to Paul Smith, where you study the way you do at Pathways. You can major in wetland conservation, study whatever you want study—to be a police officer or guide. The main reason I like Paul Smith is that you can bring your guns on campus. You are allowed to have your guns, and there is a huge lake out in front there. Wicked good fishing, good duck hunting. A really good college.

In his second 10th-grade semester, Sterling designed a project as first mate on a fishing boat off Florida, e-mailing and blogging his advisors on tasks from his "punch list" that fit the Competencies. He conducted his final exhibition on Skype and earned all his planned credits.

4. Producing Evidence of Learning

While reading books, gathering information from the Internet, conducting interviews, making films, and working in the community, students begin to gather evidence of their learning that they can include in exhibitions of their work. Reflective writing assignments based on the standards organize each semester, creating the foundation for exhibitions. After reading extensively and interviewing teachers, Justice began to assemble a lecture and lengthy essay on Renaissance painters, with illustrative paintings and annotated bibliography.

Justice (10th Grade)

[My] second project was linked to the medieval times, more precisely the Renaissance, and later the Dutch era. I like old stuff. It's cool. It's a comparison of two artists: Johannes Vermeer and the famous Leonardo da Vinci. Their styles, their paintings, are different. Leonardo was also an anatomy expert and biologist, so he could capture the human form like when you make a muscle you can see the indent of the muscle. You can see how the bones work. You can imagine the movement. That was his specialty. *Mona Lisa* was not the best example, but you can see the smile starting to form. That's the mysterious thing.

Vermeer's style makes plain things look extraordinary. He will take a simple setting. My favorite is *The Milkmaid.* Just a milkmaid making dinner for her family, pouring a jar of milk into a dish. You can imagine seeing the milk being poured out. But it was lavish in the background. He had this blue, which is now called Vermeer blue. It was really nice, using a really good mix of colors. He used something called a badger brush, which was not popular in Leonardo's time. They took the air out of a badger's stomach after they killed it. It's used for mixing tones. Like in the *Girl With a Pearl Earring*, she has a turban, her headband is bluish, and it fades into her face. Then he also has skin that fades into the shadow on the other side of her face. That's what the badger brush does.

It's not just my history and social studies credits, it also my art. So I met with Mr. Babbitt, one of art teachers here at Mount Abraham. We just went over what we would look for in a painting, and it slowly evolved from painting in general to Vermeer. He gave me these cool books about Vermeer. There is an interactive website for Vermeer. You click on a painting. They give you a little magnifying glass, and you trace it over the painting, and it will tell you how he made that. I had an assumption about the badger brush. I knew there was something out there about mixing the tone of the skin, which was bright, to a mixture for the skin with the shade over it.

In my presentation I will give brief summary of their styles; then I am going to put their paintings up there and tell them about the differences and tell them what I look for in a painting. I am going to compare *The Concert* of Vermeer against the *The Virgin and Child With Saint Anne*. Then I am going to show the most famous paintings, the *Pearl Earring* and *Mona Lisa,* two of the greatest portraits, in my opinion, of their days. To avoid looking like someone who complains, I will point out the good, the bad, and the ugly. Each painter has problems, but each has his shining moments.

I am going to try being unbiased. I do prefer Vermeer. I like the colors, the hues. I am going to try comparing style, the body, motion, and structure—the actual faces or expressions, then go into the major parts. I want to compare the situations. What's going on. In Vermeer, the woman is pouring milk into a dish. In the *Mona Lisa,* it is harder, though. I spent 2 hours just looking at this one painting. I see only the motion of the face. What is she smiling at? I don't know.

While playing football in the center of the line, Justice wrote several long papers and created a slide presentation for his final exhibition, while also building and testing medieval war machines based for credits in science and mathematical reasoning.

5. Preparing for Exhibitions

Reviewing a semester to emphasize skills and knowledge from the Competencies has proven to be a major intellectual challenge. Moving toward the end of a semester, students focus on converting the evidence they have gathered into an hourlong presentation to peers, advisors, mentors, and parents—on changes in their learning. Creating films, photos, essays, diagrams, and other media provokes students to think about the meaning of what they have done. Working with their advisor, they then examine the rubrics for the graduation competencies and organize their evidence to show they have met each of them. As he began converting the family farm to a hog raising operation, Joe saw his work as a narrative—a story—rather than an analytic essay.

Starting a Pig Farm Pig
Joe (8th Grade)

In 7th grade, I didn't like it much. I fought with my teachers every day, and I got straight Fs. I told my mother I wanted to get the dropout papers so I could drop out in 7th grade. She wasn't too happy about that. The teachers were trying to get me to do work that wouldn't help me much, in my future life. They had me learn about things I didn't want to learn about. I used to take English, history, science, and band. I kept asking them why I had to do this if I wanted to be a pig farmer. I got the work done, but I was one of the slowest kids in class. I took my time, but I was mostly just looking at a wall.

My exhibition will be on swine farming, also known as pig farming. I had to work and read books, get information off the Internet, talk to another pig farmer about tips on how to raise them. I had to build a PowerPoint, and I built a wooden model of a pigpen. In the first semester, I took on a lot of veterinarian work because we still had cows. We have a big stall, about four feet across. We hope to make two of those or three of them for pigs. I have two pigs of my own well two pregnant gilts, one boar, and a new sow. That would generate 14 piglets per sow twice a year; that's 28 piglets per year. Every 21 days she can start a new cycle. A cycle lasts five days. I am aiming for 50 to 75 swine.

I feed them twice a day, about seven pounds, usually at 6 in the morning and 4 at night. I need time do things that need to be done. I spend my days mostly in the barn helping, cleaning the pigs, feeding them. I also help my father in the field, what we have to do to get ready, because he is going into garden work after selling off the cows. So I have to help plow the field and harrow. He is helping me, and I am helping him, all the way through our years.

I get on the computer and/or write my PowerPoint every day. I upload photos and information and read more in the book. So I get more information and make a slide every day. If I have a lot of information, I make two to four slides a day. I put information on each one. Then I put pictures in. I had 25 slides in my exhibition. Next week I get my reflections back, so I start writing what else I have to do. I have done some writing about books. I have read *Guide to Raising Pigs* by Kelly Klober, who has been a pig farmer for 35 years, and he has been a 4-H leader and a pig teacher.

Reflective writing assignments based on the standards creates a structure for exhibitions. Joe used photography extensively to document the process of working with cows and then raising pigs on the family farm. He made a video film on birthing a calf, models of farm structures, and records of interviews with professionals in several areas of farming. Meanwhile, as a 10th-grade student, he had 150 pigs in the barn, and he was beginning to earn money, a new topic to develop for the next year.

6. Presenting and Revising for Grades and "Best-Work" Portfolios

Facing the end of a semester, advisors focus on helping students revise their products so they meet the Five Competencies. During exhibitions, each student presents a project for 1 hour, gathering feedback from program advisors, community mentors, friends, parents, and teachers. The exhibition is a time to celebrate work that has been done, but also to gather feedback from the audience about how to show they have earned the credits they aimed to earn. From all the feedback, a student's advisor creates a final "punch list" of changes necessary to earning credit. For the last two weeks of a semester, the advisor works with each student to make sure that revisions meet the competencies. While raising hogs, Joe kept began to see that his exhibition provided insight into his growth, changing the original story to an assessment of progress.

7. Revising for Credit

Please see Chapter 6, which addresses the mechanics of assessment as it unfolds from a formative stage to final grading.

Connecting Action to Meaning
Joe's Final Reflection

I have thought logically in many ways. One way that I had to think logically is when I had to manage the rapid growth of population in my pigs. I also have to think logically about the design and building of the pens for all the new pigs. I also have to think logically when it is time to breed my pigs and when they furrow so I can build more pens for the new ones. Another time when I have to think logically is when I have to switch the group to sell the older ones and keep all the females that year so I can keep the same amount of hogs in the barn.

I have practiced gathering, organizing, and evaluating my information in a couple of ways. One way that I organize my information is that I put all of my information on my evidence file on my website. At this time I have 12 things on it. I evaluate my information by reading it over, and if it doesn't look like good information, then I don't use it; I use my prior knowledge to evaluate my information. I have also found it useful to ask questions about my project. I have been asking questions to myself so I can keep learning about hog slaughtering.

I take the same steps when I am faced with a problem. The first thing I do is go to the Internet to see if that can help me. If the Internet can't help me, I go to my peers for help. If they can't help me, I go to the advisors. I also try to solve the problem in as many ways as I can.

I have to use creativity and imagination in many ways. The first way I use my imagination is when I had to imagine how to change the cow stalls into pigpens using my imagination. I am creative because I had to build pigpens out of wood and screws.

By having these skills, I can do a lot more things on my own. Since I can solve problems I can survive when I get out of high school. Since I can ask good questions, I can ask people or myself about my hog farming operation. Now that I am more creative, I can create and build better pens for my pigs. Since I can gather, evaluate, and organize my information, I will be able to learn new things about hog farming and make sure it is good information. I can also organize all my breeding and furrowing of my pigs.

Joe's best-work portfolio contains videos, building plans, book responses, and this reflection that he selected to show how he has met graduation competencies.

The Process Is the Learning

Pathways moved quickly away from its libertarian origins, but advisors and students are more satisfied working within guidelines than they were when on any day almost anything could happen, with or without a plan. As Russell Comstock explained, the evolution that began with the phases of a semester then began to generate scaffolding for each phase:

We have come a long way from being completely personalized and free—to our current program with enough scaffolding that helps students learn. Recently we have seen a lot of progress with students handing in work—evidence of their learning: photos, stories, movies, documentation, written work, physical art projects, much more significant than when we got in early semesters. This is a program that really leans on evidence. Because it is so open ended, we need to be able to show what students can do with open inquiry.

The road to graduation is unique to each student, following a track that no one can predict at the outset, but that grows increasingly clear as the student completes projects and designs new ones. The program serves instead as a gateway to educational opportunities throughout this small rural area. Successful projects usually depend on a network of support that connects the family, school, and local community to each student's learning path, thereby enhancing the student's ability to achieve personal goals in meaningful and relevant ways. The general structure, guidelines, schedules, and advisor check-ins take Pathways toward its aim—the capability to engage all students in learning how to manage the work of their minds, no matter what their age, prior learning, or early achievement might have been.

NAGGING QUESTIONS ABOUT STRUCTURE AND FREEDOM

1. How can we adjust the balance between free inquiry and structure in ways that students will understand and accept as they develop projects?

2. How can we prepare a whole school to tolerate inevitable mistakes as students learn to manage their own learning?

3. What is a manageable teaching load for a class period devoted to personalized advising?

4. What is the difference between learning content and learning to learn?

4

Scaffolding Personal Learning

Pathways is hard. You gotta figure out what you want to do. Then you gotta do it.

—Overheard in the halls

OVERVIEW

Free inquiry depends on a tight foundation of structure. For all students, Pathways designed a website containing competency descriptions, rubrics, punch lists, and models of successful products of individual student work so students can add their drafts, final products, and other evidence of competency to their sites. Advisors have access to student sites, and students invite others to link in. This chapter illustrates scaffolding for the *Independent Learning Competency* and provides a more extensive example of meeting the *Critical Thinking Competency*. As students gain competence and mastery of the Pathways process, advisors can put aside the scaffolding tools and let inquiry find its natural path.

Focusing on Competency

Whether for a short period or long, students in the Personalized Learning Department and Pathways need specific guidelines for project development that they can work effectively so as to gain experience and competence in any skill among the Five Competencies. When students first come to Pathways, the competencies themselves seem incomprehensible. Self-advocacy? Thinking logically? One student thought "perseverance" had something to do with the weather. The terms mean little until students use them to plan and organize their work. As a preference, young people may cling to concrete objects and actions but bypass organizing concepts that let them transfer and adapt their skills to new challenges. With the guidance of an advisor, students come to see that they can use their projects to drive learning that will be useful for a lifetime. Since the pilot semester, the Pathways team has worked to assemble enough "scaffolding" to help students learn to manage their movement toward college and work.

Through community experience, students learn directly what it means to work as a doctor, architect, weightlifter, nurse, builder, farmer, or writer. What they often fail to see is what it takes to get there: educational preparation, connections between concepts and skills, practice or ways to improve the results they are getting in their work. With regular usage, the competencies become an organizing language, providing a lens for seeing their work from a perspective that lets them improve what they do. Scaffolding personalized learning has the purpose of bridging daily work and the flexible applications that work for a lifetime so students learn how to learn.

A Pathways exhibition at which a student earns credit may include a stuffed quail, wild turkey, and an edible beaver tail as well as photos, videos, and writing about taxidermy, interview notes, and a list of books on skinning animals—with background research on bird nutrition, the physics of flight, and ecology. At first students want to see the experience itself as the only thing that counts. In time, their products may earn them some of the praise they want, but continuous self-assessment against the competencies earns them the credits they need to graduate. Finally, the skills they have learned, represented by rubrics for the Five Competencies, come to represent the value they will carry with them into the adult lives that await their arrival after graduation.

"The Space": A Website Organizing Learning

Guides for learning—competency descriptions, rubrics, punch lists (task lists), graphic organizers, feedback forms, posters explaining each competency, and a host of models that show how successful products can look—form the scaffolding students and their advisors use to prepare each section of a final exhibition. When multilayered scaffolding itself eventually became unmanageable, Josie Jordan, an English teacher/advisor and Lauren Parren, the district technology coordinator, designed personal websites so each student could manage all the materials that guide learning and all the products and assessments they accumulate to earn credit.

As Josie explained the personal sites:

> With Lauren, I created "The Space" [website organizer], everything we have designed in one location. It can be used for planning, assessing, or reflecting. Each competency has its own tab. The competency punch lists are on the competency page. The "best-work" portfolio has a tab. Each project has a tab. The punch lists, rubrics, focusing questions, examples, and models are all there. When they go to the tab for the evidence organizer for exhibition, they find out, "What have I done? What is it I should do more?" They can transition from the competency work page and look at evidence for their exhibitions, then move their best work to the portfolio section. We can't use this website organizer if it will just put out their fire. We can only use support that keeps the fire burning.

Currently, the scaffolding guides and props that help students figure out how complete a project can be found in their personal websites, available in an interactive format that can be made accessible to students, parents, teachers, and mentors—the same space where students build and revise their notes, drafts, photo, videos, and other evidence they will use to complete their best-work portfolios. Advising often takes place with a student's space open on the screen or through e-communication through the site. This chapter includes illustrations of the scaffolding guides available on "The Space" with some examples of student work.

After six semesters working with different ways to organize weeks and months of a semester, the team began to settle on a semester sequence based on the Five Competencies that enabled them to focus on one target at a time (see Chapter 3, Figure 3.2). First, students gather evidence on Independent Learning, then on Critical Thinking and Communication, and finally they review the whole semester through more conceptual perspectives, Global Citizenship and Collaboration. In a semester, the emphasis also shifts from planning and informal feedback to formal feedback and public presentation. At the same time, the focus of advising conferences moves from exploring student interests to documenting achievement for graduation credits. At each stage, advisors introduce tasks lists, definitions of the competencies, rubrics, and models for each common and self-designed task. Students use the props until they and their advisors see that they are no longer necessary, at which point students could begin to manage their own progress in consultation with others. Conventional teaching uses a schedule of topics to set the pace; personalized learning employs a succession of skills that student refine semester after semester (see Figure 4.1).

Some students choose to take on five or six projects in a semester, risking overload. Most focus in on one or two, and those often merge within a short period of time. As Figure 4.1 shows, advisors can help students see one project as the medium in which they show evidence of meeting all the competencies. Reflection on the evidence can prove that some

Figure 4.1 Flow of Support at Pathways

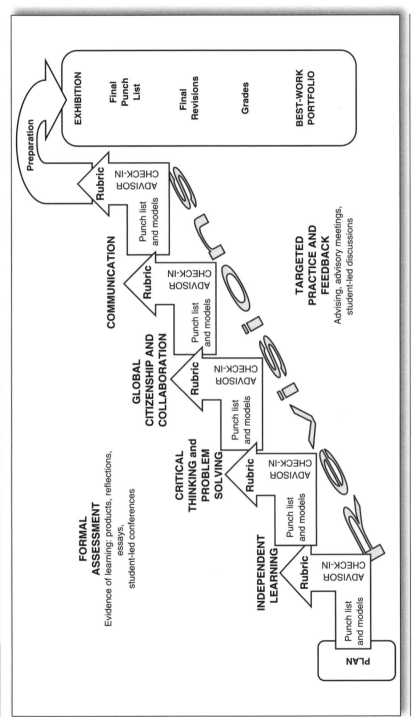

Source: Reprinted with Permission from Mount Abraham Union Middle High School, Bristol, Vermont.

knowledge of algebra helps with the spreadsheets that fore-cast profit or loss. Treating a patient can be more effective and thorough when an intern has knowledge of anatomy and chemistry. Formal classes can play a role in building knowl-edge and skill, through virtual high school, vocational/tech-nical programs, or local college classes, but so can education outside of school, such firefighting school, licensed practical nurse training at a hospital, or workshops at the YMCA. Building a personalized program for each student means helping them find sources of essential knowledge and skills in their chosen fields of interest, and "The Space" takes the clut-ter out of the process of making sense.

Designing Processes and Products

After the pilot semester made it clear that high school stu-dents need to learn how to learn, the Pathways team has revised the scaffolding props each semester. The work of con-tinuous program redesign at Pathways helps the team fit com-mon tasks to a particular group of students and develop individual tasks that also generate evidence for the competen-cies. Experience and ongoing dialogue let primitive versions of scaffolding grow more sophisticated and appropriate. Josie became the team member who took up the task of converting team discoveries into learning guides.

> You can't put a student from a mainstream classroom into student-designed learning without a transition. It is not realistic. The students are used to teacher direction. Having the structures supports them through the transition. For some students, the support soon becomes unnecessary and cumbersome. You have to create the structure but then be flexible because the program is all about personalization and students learning to manage without structure.
>
> In the team meetings, as people are sharing ideas, I am actually creating the documents that organize and articu-late those ideas. I need to see the structures that help

| Figure 4.2 | One Project Meeting Five Competencies |

Composting Tyler wants to find out whether it is possible to make a living from making compost from food waste.

Gathering Information
Tyler reviews different designs for profitable composting sites, based on aeration, bacteria growth, and the physics of efficient stockpiling; he designs a workable site.

Critical Thinking
Tyler completes a feasibility study for a composting business: capital costs, operating costs, equipment and personnel; then he projects income at three levels of success and decides he can break even in a year.

Global Citizenship
Tyler approaches the Bristol town manager, asking for room at the town dump for a composting study. He has to present to the select board. Agreement does not come easily, mostly for those directly affected. Tyler pitches his plan, complete with graphics. He gets the vote.

Tyler's Exhibition and Portfolio

Communication (Writing)
Encouraged by his mentor, Tyler works through the proposal writing process, with at least five revisions before presenting it to the Town Council. Each presentation and facet of new research leads to another revision. His last draft is clean and strong.

Composting Site
Tyler collects garbage and sets it up in a planned site at the town dump so he can sell to the community.

Independent Learning
Slowly, committed to his vision, Tyler puts aside his natural shyness and engages adults in his community. He makes numerous cold calls to those involved to set up interviews. Talking with local experts helps him build confidence for standing up in front of the community to present his ideas.

Source: Reprinted with Permission from Mount Abraham Union Middle High School, Bristol, Vermont.

students meet a goal and provide us with a basis for rapid feedback. I feared sometimes I was putting in too many boundaries and boxing things in, but then I thought, we can always expand the box. We have to be clear about what we want if we want them to create the evidence they need. The goal of the punch lists is to get them to generate enough material to meet one of the competencies.

We realized last year that students did not know how to write a reflection. So, I did a "Jane Doe" reflection and portfolio models too. Then students began to create the models for each reflection. Now, all the examples on "The Space" are by students. They can say, "That's me. That's me." Logan came up with the Collaboration punch list. Then we turned Global Citizenship completely over to the students. Simply by answering competency questions they can create their own punch lists and weekly tasks lists. Some of them don't even need the punch lists. They are already doing so much.

If you have it laid out, like a toolbox, you may not know what you need right away, but you can reach in for what you want. I got each advisor to sit next to me and help shape the site we made. I had a template, but I needed to know that the advisors could use it as we intend it to be used.

In a conventional classroom, the teacher takes responsibility for allocating and managing the available learning time. Because control over too many young people in one room can consume a lot of time in itself, classroom teachers tend to schedule the minutes tightly and keep a strong hand on the pace of a class period. In a personalized setting, the students must allocate their own time to all the tasks they face as they work toward exhibitions. Students may flounder at the beginning, wallowing without clear purpose through unconnected websites but not yet fitting experience and research into a whole idea. By Exhibition time, the hours and minutes grow deathly quiet as students read, work at their computers, or go through their punch lists. Facing burnout while taking notes, students soon learn to treat their time flexibly, putting in a half hour for independent physical education, going up to a tech lab to build their projects—or talking with friends. On the wallboard where students and advisors publicize their discoveries, one experienced student wrote, "If you are doing nothing, you must be doing something wrong." Making students aware of all the things they can do with their time is one way to ensure they are using their freedom. A wall hanging such as "What do I do with My Time" (Figure 4.3) can remind them of their choices. Keeping an extensive "do list" organized around the competencies also ensures that they always have choices.

Asking for adult help is probably not the predominant inclination of young people who are fighting to expand their freedom. Some students can see asking for help as asking for unwanted attention. Some do not have much experience working closely with older people. Pathways students are surrounded by adults who are ready to help but who try not to step in until they are asked or when intervention is necessary to keep students moving forward. The advisor role includes scheduling meetings called "check-ins." Parents often play a crucial role in supporting an inquiry project, consulting, gathering materials, or just driving to work sites and events. Faculty mentors guide students toward resources in the subject areas. Community mentors may have to develop the ability to see the questions that an intern is not asking until students get used to making telephone calls, writing e-mail messages, interviewing experts by phone, or talking with people in their field of interest. In most situations, the advisor and community liaison help students discover the resources that are available.

Managing time stands out as an obstacle for new students, who can make little progress until they take control of what they are doing. Gerrie Heuts, the community liaison who helps students work with their community mentors, sees self-management as the immediate and enduring task they face, but also the with the greatest payoff in adult life. Gerrie hears about their struggles as she drives from site to site.

Figure 4.3   So What DO I Do With My Time?

One-on-One Time With My Advisor
Talk with my advisor about what I'm doing
Figure out what I need
Plan projects and set up my schedule
Look over my contract
Prepare for my Exhibition Presentations
Talk about my Work Log
Talk about my community engagement
Talk about changes in my contract and projects
Get feedback on my work
Talk

Community Time
Meet with my community mentor
Shadow someone in my interest area
Work a job
Work on special events
Provide services to those in need
Collect information from community members
Plan a community event
Do an internship
Do an apprenticeship

Time Working on Projects
Work on my computer to get information and create new ideas
Make a video, website or blog
Clean up stuff for my portfolio
Develop my exhibition presentation
Read, write, and work with numbers
Assemble information
Make tables, draw graphs, or find solutions

Class Time
Take classes at Mt. Abe
Take classes at a college
Take an Internet class
Go to seminars at Pathways
Attend a tutorial

Lunch
Eat and rest
Learn to play an instrument
Shoot some hoops
Walk
Run
Reflect

Time With Advisory Team
Collaborate with others
Design group projects
Plan trips and events
Update the team on my projects
Ask for ideas to improve the work
Figure out more projects
Set up discussions
Help keep the space neat

Source: Reprinted with permission from Mount Abraham Union Middle High School, Bristol, Vermont.

What comes to mind with this kind of learning is the challenge they have with themselves. Figuring out if they can learn this way, independent and free flowing. Before going out to the field, the challenge is to organize and motivate themselves. The younger students are usually less organized about having the materials they need. The more mature students can overcome this challenge more easily, gathering materials, checking in with their mentors—checking out with me.

Then, they face another other challenge in the fear of speaking with adults, working with adults, from the first "cold call" to working on the job. Any relationship takes time to develop; so does the one between a student and a mentor. It can take more than six weeks in a semester. It took more than a year and half for Sterling and Brian Anderson, the blacksmith, before they became comfortable together at the forge.

LEARNING TO LEARN INDEPENDENTLY

Recognizing the importance of self-management to personalized learning, the Pathways advisors set up Independent Learning as a separate graduation competency, on an equal plane with other academic skills, and the first competency for each semester. Having identified engagement, perseverance, self-advocacy, time management, accountability, and productivity as indicators of Independent Learning, they designed the focusing questions, criteria, and achievement to guide student planning during project development. As part of their response to the punch list on Independent Learning, students write a reflection essay on their experience organized around the criteria for that competency, using a model developed by the advisors and other students to create a picture of how a reflection might look (see Figure 4.5 Model: Independent Learning Skills Reflection).

The Independent Learning Competency has become the only target of the Middle School mini Pathways course.

Figure 4.4 Independent Learning Rubric

Student: Project Assessed: Date:

Assessed by: self/peer/teacher/other

Indicator	Getting Started	Developing	Proficient	Mastery	Far Exceeds Expectations
Perseverance *How do I handle obstacles?*	Stops trying after first obstacles; Dismisses projects when difficulties arise; Requires daily coaching from advisors	Stalls on projects when problems arise; Will keep trying if advisor helps	Makes an honest effort to solve problems and move through obstacles; Tries to problem-solve	Works hard to get through difficulties; Regularly tries new strategies or different approaches	Motivated to solve problems; Welcomes challenges as new opportunities
Evidence:					
Inquiry *What do I do to generate ideas and questions to pursue?*	Relies on an advisor to generate ideas; Shows little interest; Doesn't consider own interests or surroundings for inspiration	Looks to own interests to propose ideas; Makes questions with advisor's help	Keeps track of interests and ideas for potential projects; Researches ideas to find questions of interest	Regularly reflects on personal interests and surroundings to generate ideas; Reaches out to colleagues and community for inspiration	Updates and maintains a list of current and future ideas and questions Listens for opportunities; Uses research to generate new ideas

Indicator	Getting Started	Developing	Proficient	Mastery	Far Exceeds Expectations
Time Management *How do I plan ahead and budget my time?*	Evidence:				
	Has no plan; Does not consider how best to spend time; Not aware of deadlines	Plans moment to moment; Considers deadlines when prompted by advisor	Plans for a day; Schedules a few events in the week; Aware of some deadlines and makes schedule or list of tasks and Ideas with advisor	Considers long-term goals and deadlines to independently makes a weekly plan; Breaks down weekly deadlines into daily goals	Makes daily, weekly, and monthly plans; Sets a realistic timeframe; Checks personal schedule daily to determine activities; Looks ahead to avoid conflicts
Accountability *How do I follow through with tasks, appointments, errands, etc.?*	Evidence:				
	Does not look at or work on project task lists; Misses appointments; Changes destinations	Only works on project task lists with advisor direction; Goes to appointments when reminded; Sometimes takes detours en route	Works on project task lists on own; Remembers and attends own appointments	Systematically completes tasks from project lists; Prepares ahead for appointments without advisor prompting	Completes project task lists as a starting point; Plans ahead for appointments; Follows up with thank-you notes when appropriate

(Continued)

Figure 4.4 (Continued)

Indicator	Getting Started	Developing	Proficient	Mastery	Far Exceeds Expectations
	Evidence:				
Demonstrates Learning *How can I show my learning?*	Does not process or show results of learning	Can describe own learning but regularly needs advisor prompting to create items that show learning	Independently creates products that support and document learning at least once a week; Plans for exhibition and regularly updates plan	Creates items that illustrate and display learning accurately; Records evidence that demonstrates learning on a daily basis	Daily activity results in useful and interesting products; Documents learning during project work; Expresses knowledge clearly
	Evidence:				
Self-Advocacy *How do I seek out help when I need it?*	Avoids advisor contact; Does not acknowledge difficulties or obstacles	When asked will discuss questions or concerns	Shares concerns or questions during scheduled advisor meetings	Regularly looks for advisor to ask questions or get assistance; Anticipates scheduled advisor meetings	Initiates regular appointments with advisors, mentors, and teachers; Independently accesses library and community resources

92

Source: Reprinted with Permission from Mount Abraham Union Middle High School, Bristol, Vermont.

Figure 4.5 Model: Independent Learning Skills Reflection

1. **Purpose:** To think to myself, and share with advisors, how I've been using or developing Independent Learning skills.

2. **Organization:** Look at each of the Indicators of Independent Learning one by one.

3. **Details:** I have to use examples from my work to show how I've been doing.

4. **Tone:** Personal but with professional language.

5. **GUM:** I should make sure I don't have typos or mistakes that make it hard to understand my ideas.

──────────────── **MODEL** ────────────────

Make your first sentence one that summarizes your work so far.

This semester I have some new ideas I'm looking at, and some old topics I'm trying to continue or develop more. I'm excited to try Zumba dance classes and work to improve my writing with a professional's feedback. I will keep helping my friend David Lipkin to remodel and paint some rooms in his house, and I will look toward some spring landscaping or gardening.

Mention your key project plans.

It's interesting how each semester goes so differently. I haven't felt a lot of momentum compared to the fall when I was busy. So looking at *Inquiry*, I have not done as well as I could. I've been more dependent on advisors to brainstorm ideas, and I haven't researched very much on my own. Gerrie connected me with Zumba classes and a writer, John Elder, in town who said he would look at my work. I got those ideas from an advising meeting with Russell. I'm glad to do those activities, but I didn't find them myself.

Think about and share how you've been doing.

Use specific examples.

Share what you've been trying to do too.

The past two weeks I've been doing a lot of *Perseverance* to get the punch list done. I have worked to stay focused and not get distracted with others. For example, one time when the room was too loud I went next door to get some work done. I also persevered trying to find the Zumba schedule. Bristol Fitness doesn't have its own website, so after much searching

Be honest. Use a personal tone.

(Continued)

Figure 4.5   (Continued)

online, I had to make a phone call to find out where their schedules are listed.

Start each paragraph with introduction of topic.

I know one skill that I always do well is **Self-Advocacy**. I get bored just cruising the Web or sitting around, so I'm always asking the advisors for ideas of what I can do next. For example, Russell helped me think of garden research and planning so I can still do landscape work even though its winter. I'm also good at **Organization** because I keep track of all the websites I use on www.Diigo.com. It will make my annotated bibliography easy to do. I'm also good at keeping all my papers in my own folder and the one here in the room. You won't ever find my papers floating around.

Again, use specific examples.

Since it's the beginning of the semester, I don't have significant **Demonstration** completed, but I do know what I will have to show in a few weeks. For Zumba, I will have my dance log and reflection after each class. For landscaping, I will have my research notes and garden plans, and for my writing I will have multiple drafts and feedback from John Elder. I also will be taking before-and-after pictures of my friend's mudroom and library.

Use phrases to transition.

If you don't have it now, say what you plan to do.

For me to get all of this done, I will have to use **Time Management**. I like to write my appointments and classes down in a small calendar I keep in my bag. I also met with Josie and made deadlines for my different writing assignments. I write these down too, in my calendar, and I plan which nights or days I will do what. I find that I won't really do the work, or I'll put it off, if I don't have set dates by which I have to finish my work. That's why I asked Russell to give me a deadline for a garden plan that I will have to show him.

Show self-reflection or analysis.

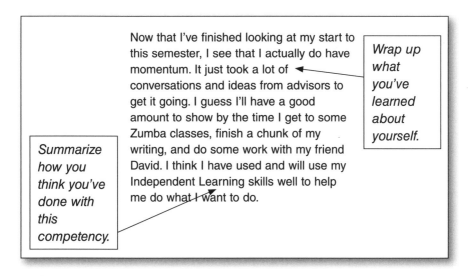

Summarize how you think you've done with this competency.

Now that I've finished looking at my start to this semester, I see that I actually do have momentum. It just took a lot of conversations and ideas from advisors to get it going. I guess I'll have a good amount to show by the time I get to some Zumba classes, finish a chunk of my writing, and do some work with my friend David. I think I have used and will use my Independent Learning skills well to help me do what I want to do.

Wrap up what you've learned about yourself.

Source: Reprinted with permission from Mount Abraham Union Middle High School, Bristol, Vermont.

Justice, whom you may remember from the comparison of Jan Vermeer and Leonardo da Vinci, has learned to reflect deeply on his progress in managing multiple projects.

Justice (10th Grade)

I have had to learn time management. I was used to being on a schedule, 80-minute classes with a break. I was just relying on the teachers when I had to change subjects from English to math. When I went to Pathways, they said you have to manage your own time. We are not going to rag on you. We will give you help. That first semester, I was not used to the privileges. Time management is a privilege. Free roaming. You have your path. The computers and technology we are allowed to use. We are allowed to reach out beyond Mt. Abe. Some branch out to Middlebury College or VTV [Vermont Technical College], a lot of other colleges. You can have a mentor outside the high school. That's a big, big privilege.

Second semester, I started really planning my time. I plan time working on my projects, reading and writing—and just doing things I just like to do, like writing, literature. I write on the keyboard or paper if something pops into my head to write down. One of my advisors, Josie, told me to read *Leonardo's Notebook.* I have a notebook in my backpack. If I have an idea I write it down, even if it's the roughest idea, I write it down. I just write stuff at random, something on the first page will show up among the last essay. I go back to the notes. That's what Leonardo did.

Having focused on independent learning in his first semester, Justice was able see the growth of his intellectual approach over the longer term:

Learning what I didn't like to learn? Boring! Tune out. Don't pay attention. Just read. I used to read more than anyone else—at the most inappropriate times. I still do in English. I like to write. I like to read. I like to do things that I like—to learn. I have no problems learning my necessaries, like math or the English language or grammar. But if I am not interested in Greek mythology, I am not interested in Greek mythology.

For a person like Justice, self-awareness leads to increased control, the "metacognitive" ability to recognize how he uses his mind and make adjustments to get a better result—a new idea or a better strategy.

I just think about what I think. Hey, I have a new idea about a project. You are going to think. Why? You continue tracing that. You start thinking, why did I think of that? What triggered that? Backtracking to what caused it, then going forward, you have to find a track. Or I lose track. I have to start with a story line, then branch off into more interesting things. I like to stay on a story line, and then back up. If you lose your train of thought, it's going to break. Then, you can't remember. That's a really bad feeling. You've got to make sure you stay on track. Don't jump off the train.

Pathways aims for self-awareness at this depth for all students, but it does not come easily to those who have not practiced and reflected on independent learning—and grown to see self-direction as their road to freedom.

As they work on their projects, students look at wall hangings of competencies and questions as reference points, letting them see a larger framework for their work. About half of a punch list consists of common tasks for all students, such as developing an annotated bibliography or writing a reflective essay. Advisors also design specific tasks for a student's punch list based on the specifics of a project and level of competency (see Figure 4.6).

Learning Critical Thinking and Problem Solving: An Illustration

Because personalized learning aims to prepare students to direct their own lives, we have to emphasize the processes adults use to solve ill-defined problems, rather than yes/no problems, and move effectively toward workable solutions. Young adults have a harder time distinguishing between simple problems, which disappear after they plug in a simple solution, and complex problems, which will not yield to a quick swipe of the hand. Project planning poses that kind of problem. When they have recognized problem solving as a definable process for ill-defined situations, they gradually become more interested in understanding problems than avoiding them. When they have solved several complex problems successfully, they feel that struggling with complexity and coming up with defensible solutions are actually enjoyable. Students need to learn problem solving as a strategy they can adopt and adapt when situations arise that will respond only to a conscious strategy.

Young people do not tend to see themselves as aggressive problem solvers, even though they may have been solving complex problems all of their lives. Coming up through grade school, they may see the word "problem" as laden with negative implications: "Problem child," "Don't make this a problem," and, "What's the problem, here?" "Are you going to give me a problem?" For younger people, the word

Figure 4.6   Words Let You See the World

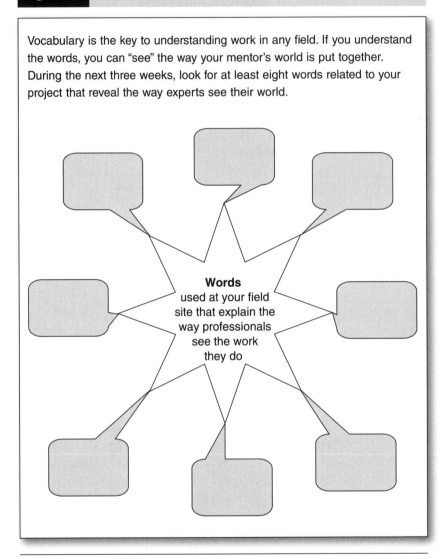

Vocabulary is the key to understanding work in any field. If you understand the words, you can "see" the way your mentor's world is put together. During the next three weeks, look for at least eight words related to your project that reveal the way experts see their world.

Words
used at your field site that explain the way professionals see the work they do

Source: Reprinted with permission from Mount Abraham Union Middle High School, Bristol, Vermont.

"problem" leads as often to the word "punishment" as the word "solution," so we should understand when they do not respond enthusiastically when "problems" come up in their work with teachers. From an adult perspective, the word is much more positive, suggesting that a situation has been identified that we can change for the better:

- If you want to give someone a gift, give her a problem to solve.
- Problems are our friends. Problems are our teachers.
- Failed again? Looks like we face a higher-quality problem.

Because solving problems may be the defining activity in adult life, high school students have to learn to see the term essential to gaining control over their lives.

We should not be surprised that younger people are not that good at solving complex problems. And, not surprisingly, young people often solve problems impulsively. They wreck a car, get caught up in drugs, get pregnant by mistake, or go to jail more frequently than older people, without necessarily seeing that a problem exists. The problem-solving graphic is there to slow down impulsive leaps. It splits an invisible process into pieces that students can use to see where they are and plan where they want to go.

The illustration that follows includes a series of props developed by the Pathways team, aiming to instill the ability to solve problems in people who need both strategies and practice. It features steps that identify problem solving as a manageable process; a schematic showing problem solving as a series of steps; a rubric that advisors can use to help students see how they are progressing as problem solvers; models of problem solving that fit the rubric; a punch list of assignments that prepare students to recognize and plan solutions; and a feedback sheet that shows students what they need to do to master the skills. With guided practice, students can begin to manage multifaceted strategies for problems that are embedded in others, derived from distant causes, multicausal, or just intricate. The ability to solve ill-defined problems—global warming, finding a career, raising children, or designing a house, for example—depends on learning to work flexibly inside the problem, changing tactics

Figure 4.7   Problem Solving as a Critical Thinking Competency

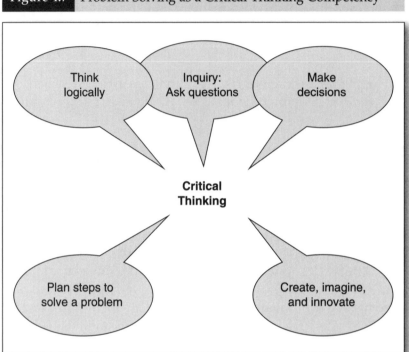

Source: Reprinted with Permission from Mount Abraham Union Middle High School, Bristol, Vermont.

as parts of a solution emerge, transforming remaining problems, and calling for further thought. Problem solving is attached to the larger competency called "Critical and Creative Thinking" (Figure 4.7).

The bubble map represents a concept of problem solving as a part of critical thinking, but it does not represent the "how-to" of the process that would let students design a strategy or adapt their approach. The Problem-Solving Guide lets students see their progress within a set of phases. Looking at the guide for problem solving in Figure 4.8, some students comment that the schema seems both self-evident and excessively mechanical, as befits its origins in the worlds of business, engineering, and the military. It may not become useful until students hit an

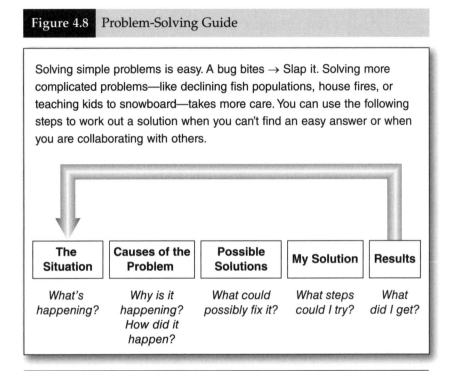

Figure 4.8   Problem-Solving Guide

Solving simple problems is easy. A bug bites → Slap it. Solving more complicated problems—like declining fish populations, house fires, or teaching kids to snowboard—takes more care. You can use the following steps to work out a solution when you can't find an easy answer or when you are collaborating with others.

The Situation	Causes of the Problem	Possible Solutions	My Solution	Results
What's happening?	Why is it happening? How did it happen?	What could possibly fix it?	What steps could I try?	What did I get?

Source: Reprinted with permission from Mount Abraham Union Middle High School, Bristol, Vermont.

intellectual wall or find they have to collaborate with others in solving a problem. To collaborate with others, they have to communicate about their approach to a shared task, and they need a defined game board. The process guide also provides a basic outline for their reflection essay on problem solving.

Punch lists: Students may not recognize the role of problem solving in their projects until they work through assignments that make the process palpable—and perhaps even enjoyable. The punch lists give them specific tasks to complete by a set date, before which they schedule a "check-in" with their advisor to find out how close they are to meeting competency requirements.

Rubrics with criteria: To prepare an exhibition that meets the requirements for credits, Pathways students have to describe

Figure 4.9   Critical Thinking Punch List

Why practice, know, and identify your Critical Thinking Skills?

A. You'll know what you're good at and how you can get better.
B. If something is not working, you can try something else.
C. You can work with others to know a sequence and move together in order to get a task done.

Punch List #2: Critical Thinking Skills
Due October

1. Analyze the good and bad of a situation you've encountered. You could make:
   a. A chart
   b. A diagram
   c. A reflection
   d. A collage with interpretation provided
      • Upload to your Evidence File.

2. Attend a Bias and Perspective seminar.
   • Complete practice exercise and upload to your Evidence File.

3. Find or create a new or better idea about something in your field of interest (i.e., find and use a better software program to make a movie or make a new tool to use while welding).
   • Show what you make and upload to your Evidence File.

4. Imagine you had $500 and transportation provided to pursue your interest next semester. What would you do? What project would you create?

5. Choose a problem you have had during one of your learning activities.
   a. Describe the situation.
   b. Explain how the problem happened.
   c. Describe more than one possible solution.

> d. Which one was the best solution?
> e. Describe the outcomes and results.
>   - This can be a chart, a list, a reflection, a PowerPoint, etc.
>   - Upload to your Evidence File.
>
> 6. Have at least 10 files (including ones assigned on this punch list) uploaded into your Project Site Evidence File. Upload photos, interviews, film clips, work logs, reflections, journal entries, etc., by October.

Source: Reprinted with permission from Mount Abraham Union Middle High School, Bristol, Vermont.

and show their work, but they also connect what they have done to the competencies and criteria that the Pathways team will use in a final assessment. The rubrics accomplish two important tasks: They introduce a vocabulary that students can use to describe their learning, rather than the work itself, and they portray a ladder from little progress to exceptional achievement in a way that shows students how to "climb" toward excellence as a semester unfolds.

By the end of a semester, students can see their work in light of the criteria that the team will use to assign credit, and they can use words that define the ineluctable workings of their own minds so they can talk about developing intellectual skills with parents, friends, and peers.

PROBLEM SOLVING WITH HANDS

S.J. (9th Grade)

S.J. came to Pathways because she was thinking of becoming an architect. She was also curious about design and aesthetics as a part of the process, with housing and community projects as a particular focus. Thinking ahead about the best future choice for herself, she had identified the University of California, Berkeley, as the kind of college she should aim to enter. To check out that choice as a 9th-grade student, 14 years old, she chose to do an internship in landscape design and architecture, working beside two local architects who were designing workable plans for real clients. She also enrolled in a design technology class at the high school, a course that included house design.

S.J.'s internship with the architects reinforced her coursework, but at the firm where she worked as a member of a team, another dimension and another Pathways competency. She participated in three contracted projects, a pool house with a model, a draft landscape for a local college, and a plan and model for an inn near the ski slopes. The plans clearly showed improvement in skill, coached into motion through daily interactions with her community mentors, Katie and Peter, in their drafting area. Both mentors had made a conscientious effort to push her past simple drafts and models toward the larger and more flexible world of design. S.J. successfully designed a house for a mouse in the high school technology course, but at Pathways, she also earned credits by expanding the scope of her inquiry to include science, English, and social studies. Her Pathways portion of her first semester depended on completing all the punch-list tasks and following the rubrics to show competence in an exhibition and portfolio. In her interview, she explained how she discovered she could do whatever she would want.

> At the beginning of Pathways, I didn't understand the scope of what I was going to do or how I would earn the core credits I need, in math, science, and English. So, then I saw I could research the history of architecture. There is English in there. I can write it, and I can figure out the science. I started doing my internship, and I saw, I get it. I can do whatever I want, and things I do with it will earn the credits. So, I can focus in on what I want to do. I want to build buildings and get better at what I do.

Her reflective paper, an assignment on her Pathways punch list, used the criteria for critical thinking and problem solving to show she had met the competency.

S.J.'s Reflective Essay on Problem Solving

In building a house for a mouse, I guess starting out with a basic idea helps. When you are building a model, you figure out the basic idea, what it will be for. Where will the rooms be? You give yourself a couple of ideas. Any design! I could be thinking a gingerbread house. A block of cheese house? I thought hamster hall. What kind of house would a mouse live in? Then, I was talking with my parents, and they said, what about a geodesic dome. I had never heard of it before. I wanted to do that. It sounded so cool. It sounds really challenging, but I want to try it. But the question was, "How am I going to make a dome?"

One problem I encountered when I started to make my geodesic dome was that the house could only have a 6 × 8 inches of property. My mouse house was going to be a dome, so I didn't know what my radius was going to be. I decided that if I knew what the perimeter was then I could just make the circumference of the circle the same as the perimeter of the rectangle. Unfortunately, after fixing that problem, more occurred, but I was prepared to solve them all with confidence.

At the top of a geodesic dome there is a place to put a pentagon. I had my base and put together all of my dome, but the pentagon didn't fit in the space where it was supposed to go. I started to freak out but told myself to calm down and find a solution. So after I contemplated my choices I decided to go with the window—it seemed simple and neat—plus geo domes are very energy-efficient homes, so if I had a large source of natural light, I would need less lamps and therefore less electricity is used.

When I had all of the walls put up, the dome didn't fit on top of it. This time because I had already encountered so many problems, I didn't immediately go into freak-out mode; I went into problem-solving mode. I considered many solutions, like, do I redo all of the walls to be the perfect shape, or do I not have any walls, or do I just trim them until they fit? I was stuck; there wasn't one solution that was the obvious choice. So, I thought about what to do, and I decided to trim as I went. After all the walls were up I realized not one wall touched the ceiling. It made sense, though, because if a geodesic dome is supposed to be energy efficient, then having the walls not touch the ceiling would help the hot or cold air circulate around the rooms.

As I encountered problems I learned to solve them without even realizing I was solving them. Problems will occur, but knowing how to solve them fast without having to always ask for help will help me later on in life. All the problems that I had to solve for my applied architecture project probably made my project turn out better, because I think my project came out better than I thought it would (I'm going to be a pro at problem solving). Working on my applied architecture project was not just important for that class but also important for what I have been researching in Pathways and architecture.

In our interview, S.J. recognized that the formal step-by-step procedure also created a structure for her writing, but she knew that her personal approach to solving problems was not linear in form. She described her many trials and errors, but also interjected the place of inspiration, creativity, and vision in architectural design.

What I think is creative, you may not think is creative. It's individuality.

I am happy. I like it. I think I feel like a put a lot of detail into it. It's me, and I look at it and I think, "If I was a mouse, I would want to live there."

—S.J., November 2011

At the end of the semester, S.J. included both the design course and internship in her exhibition, with video interview with her mentors, as well as the reflections, reading, and other evidence of learning. Her task was to explain the work she

had done in terms of the Mount Abraham graduation competencies. Eight students attended the event, as well as three of
her teachers, her parents, two mentors from the architecture
firm, three advisors, the associate superintendent, the district
technology coordinator, and three Pathways advisors, each of
whom wrote feedback for her main advisor to make into a
new punch-list for credit.

"How did you separate your coursework from Pathways?"
an advisor asked.

"I didn't. I just took on the biggest challenges," she said.

USING THE TOOLS IN ADVISING

Scaffolding alone does not do the job. Advisors make the process work. They look for progress in student work each week
and introduce language provided by the rubrics to promote
self-correction. The advisory "check-in" has proven to be
essential to any scaffolding, a mixture of listening, commenting, and guiding students toward success in their projects. At
a "check-in," students bring their punch list with products
they are developing to meet a competency, and the advisor
helps them see where they are on the rubrics.

Caroline: This week, we started off with advisor check-ins.
In those meetings, we checked progress, and then we asked
them to bring the Independent Learning punch list, and we
planned to go through the rubric, a formative assessment.
We talked to them about where they needed to progress.
They were all very accepting. No kids resisted. We were
giving them feedback instead of a grade. Here's a snapshot
of where you are and where you need to be. If they get
proficient in a competency area, they get the credit.
Explaining that you need to show evidence to get credit
gives them the choice.

Starting with the rubric makes them better at searching
and showing evidence. The rubric makes them look first at
where they have been successful—and where they are

missing evidence. I don't feel that any of the kids I worked with went away feeling overwhelmed. Most had done 70–80 percent of the work. The feedback was targeted, framing the conversation around expectations. The standards were right in front of them.

I tell them up front, my expectation is that you will continue to grow in the areas where you have not shown evidence yet. We are seeing that when you are very clear and when you give them feedback, they do respond. "Here's the standard. Here's where you are. Here's what you need to do to get there." They see that they still have time to work on it. It's not a one-time thing. As a team, we are pushing the load back to them. We work through each of the rubrics before exhibitions.

Experienced students provide scaffolding for others who are just beginning to develop skills within a competency area. When the Pathways team is having its weekly meeting, the students go to the classroom next door to work—or to join a discussion run by another Pathways student with an interest in leadership, teaching, or just learning to be helpful. As Caroline has said, not everyone will exceed high standards at the end of a semester, but all of them can learn more effectively and show how they do it.

The scaffolding provides advisors with opportunities to show students how they are doing—and how they could do better. To exploit the advantages of "rapid feedback," personalized learning relies more on daily assessment than on daily instruction. When advisors keep the flow of feedback constant, students continue revising their work to meet standards, so they do not have dead time in their schedules. Reliance on feedback puts more pressure on teachers and students to keep records so they can track their work. The more that students take responsibility for their own websites, the more time the faculty can spend working directly with them in a supportive rather than corrective mode. Regular check-ins can then focus on what it will take to finish a successful project and accumulate credits toward graduation. In an ideal state, both students and advisors develop an interest in making both formative and summative feedback flow smoothly—while shifting the burden of assessment toward students, who, after all, are the ones doing the learning.

LEAVING THE SCAFFOLD BEHIND

Scaffolding provides perceptible rigor for the Personal Learning Department and Pathways, but the purpose of scaffolding is not to constrain creativity and freedom. Scaffolding demystifies invisible processes and lets students practice meeting standards so their work achieves high quality. During check-ins, they mark the roadway to success. Increasingly, students practice independently as they become ready to do so. Then, they create their own punch lists and use the rubrics to organize their own work. Finally, after two or three semesters, many have adapted their approach so they meet standards without extra support. Then advisors may offer a bit of feedback or new options, knowing that a student can revise for final presentations on her own, landing at the high end of the competency scales. At that point, advisor check-ins become personal conversations about progress and any new choices that may be popping up along the trail. Using a tight structure to learn free inquiry is not a paradox after all. Each piece of scaffolding becomes a ladder that students can use to ascend toward proficiency while gathering clear evidence of growth.

NAGGING QUESTIONS ABOUT STRUCTURE

1. How much structure do students need? How much freedom?

2. Is it better to assess products or processes?

3. What are the risks of maintaining flexibility among tasks, products, schedules, and competency targets for each student?

4. What should we do about a student who remains unproductive for a semester?

5. What barriers would prevent teachers from focusing on process competencies rather than content acquisition?

5

Integrating School and Community

People who want to explore interests that are not available in school, or who want to get a feel for what their dream job would be like, they don't have a chance to explore that in school. Kids see how much work they have to do to get to that point or to be more realistic—or discover new things they are interested in.

—Student reflection

OVERVIEW

Personalized learning cannot develop if it is constrained by the walls of a high school. When it comes to introducing young people to adult roles, the local community has more resources than any school. Helping kids build beneficial connections with community mentors requires the full-time attention of a community liaison who can also help students take on increasingly complex tasks over successive semesters. Community mentors should strive to help a student fit in and contribute to the work setting, recognizing that they may have to sacrifice some of their own workplace effectiveness by guiding a young person. Advisors must help students understand the connection between experience in their local setting with citizenship on a global scale.

WHY LEAVE CAMPUS?

Experience in the community provides a way for young people to narrow the gap between the real and the ideal worlds. Pathways defines community as membership in the larger world, but students, who have little experience in that world, need to start somewhere small so they can continue their journey outward with increasing confidence. Disappointments may blunt or redirect first hopes, but untested hope still propels them outward from the school to the community. Although raw experience modifies their search, young people in any adult setting expand their self-awareness and build skills and knowledge that will prove useful, whatever direction they may take next. Personalized learning succeeds when adults help students refine their interests, assess their dreams, and take on challenges in the community so they increasingly understand what they want and how to get there.

Over the school years, learning moves mainly from the inside out, and adolescence is the time when young people feel the most pressure to take great leaps from dependency to independence, but few discover in high school a permanent place in the social web. Indeed, most will spend another decade after their formal education has ended making a place for themselves in the community of adults. But adolescence is a time when they can find a path from self-absorption to broader concerns, from questions about themselves to questions about others and from knowledge acquisition to the application of knowledge. Paradoxically, their determined quest for personal freedom leads to the discovery of mutuality, interdependence, and responsibility for others.

RIDING WITH THE WIZARD

Gerrie Heuts, community liaison for the Personalized Learning Department, conducts her coaching and advising from the driver's seat of an all-wheel-drive Subaru.

> I feel like the Wizard of Oz, out behind the curtain. I have to pull something out for each kid, to find a place for each one, to process it all, to stay in contact with the mentor and help them reflect on his or her role.

For a community to become part of a secondary school, somebody has to connect students to appropriate mentors, coach them in the ways of work, and solve the problems that inevitably arise when adolescents head out into new relationships with adults.

Gerrie works out problems and clarifies purpose with whoever sits next to her in the car.

- Last week, three kids were all dying to find a place to put a snowboard park. So, we got in the car and drove down past the sand pit, around the corner and into the industrial park. We looked at four or five places. They began to believe it was possible. A lot of times they do not believe their ideas are possible—because of all the restrictions they have faced at school and home.
- Niko was feeling disconnected from the music group in school because he went down to the Votec Center in Middlebury last year. At Mount Abraham, there are rednecks, firemen, computer geeks, married couples, the hippie group—and the music group. Everybody wants to find a place. Niko said the other day that he felt isolated. He had lost the gravitation of his group.
- Sammy said, "For the last three years I have done a lot of things. I became a blacksmith, making a lot of things, knives, and chimney tools. I am selling them for a good

price." He thought he had become a blacksmith. His mentor would say that he has a whole lot to learn. Now Sammy is saying, "I am going to be a duck hunter."

- "How am I going to get an A in this class?" Gabby asked—a ninth grader. "I really want to get an A+. I want to go to Berkeley." She is working with an architect. She loves it, but she asked me, "How can I get a midterm grade on this?" They try to equate performance with grades rather than personal competence.

- There is so much one-on-one in this program, people who care what you do, people who try to connect things to ideas. One of the challenges is learning the language: critical thinking, perseverance. Punctuality? One of the kids thought it was the dot at the end of a sentence. That blocked him. "What is 'punctual'?" The language is a challenge.

- I said, "Calvin, do you know what a transcript is?" No. Along with this new language, we ask them to make all kinds of decisions—but they don't understand credits and transcripts. Many have never thought about going to college. What do "credits" mean if you are not going on to college?

- Gary has to get the idea that writing a reflection after a day in the woods is English. That's English. Developing a plan for a snowboard terrain park is math, and critical thinking. The challenge is to make the association between what they are doing and the credits they are supposed to earn for learning. The parents don't understand either.

Ideally, internships over several semesters link together to form a smooth trajectory. Jason began eighth grade at Pathways with no firm sense of what he aimed to do. His demeanor was passive and shy, but his occasional comments revealed that he was also very observant. Meeting with Gerrie every other day during the early weeks gave him a chance to think and watch others leave for internships, so she was surprised and pleased one day when he said that he was interested in working with the Bristol Road Crew. She set him up for 3 hours per day, twice a week, at the town garage, which shelters trucks, plows, and other tools of road maintenance. Jason joyfully discovered he could be part of the team if he worked hard with the veterans, filling holes and pulling brush. After going out with the crew regularly on road maintenance jobs, plowing and clearing ditches, he began spending a great deal of time in the garage itself, going through each truck on routine maintenance—next to others who were already experts. Trucks, tools, techniques. Within two years, Jason had created his own small business: advertising, a truck, chainsaw, tractor, tools, and a business partner—generating further projects and plenty of work in the community. His pathway was pretty straight. Others are not.

One student in a personalized program at Mount Abraham first aspired to be a large-animal trainer. She began an internship at a local horse farm—spreading hay and mucking stalls. The next semester, she thought that healing large animals might be more exciting and less smelly, so she traveled the county with a large animal veterinarian, giving shots and putting down the sickest of the critters. Gruesome work. The next year she focused on personal expression, dance, and choreography, to some acclaim, but she also discovered there was little work available to a dancer. As a senior, she took on the sciences in general and went to college in marine biology. She now practices law in Boston. In the best sense, her wide-ranging explorations led her to understand places she would not have chosen at the outset. The rate at which young people redirect their effort can be astounding, but "changing your mind" is just "learning" by another name, the central purpose of Pathways and the Personalized Learning Department.

Each student comes to Pathways and the Personalized Learning Department with unique hopes. Each has distinctive fears. Each is wrestling with a particular set of problems at home and at school. Community mentors stir in their own idiosyncrasies. A community liaison has to navigate the unruly flow of unpredictable events, from crisis to accomplishment, so inquiry continues, and community connections survive. She has to act like a politician, counselor, administrator, fixer, promoter, and friend in a pattern that shifts every time she picks up the phone or climbs into her car. She may travel to the community college, an art studio, a wetland game preserve, and a local tourist business in one day, knowing that she may have an entirely different itinerary the next morning. At Pathways, Gerrie Heuts uses her magic to introduce young people to the adult world. Gerrie takes them from where they are to what's next, advising all the way.

Gerrie was not a teacher when she assumed the role of community liaison at Pathways. She had been the director of recreation for Bristol and the Five Towns area. Prior to that, she had run a store and a bakery. Over many years working in the community, she had developed an enormous network of friends and acquaintances. She might not be able to identify a fitting mentor after one interview with a student, but she did know whom to ask about options for any student looking for experience related to personal interests. Often, students do not come to her with specific requests, only with vague inklings. Her job is not to satisfy their curiosity and fulfill their dreams, but to begin their exploration and then find the next step. There is no end to that task.

CONNECTING WITH A COMMUNITY MENTOR

Community mentors do more than explain their work, show how it is done, and make room for projects designed by high school students. They stand at a gate separating young adults from adult freedom and responsibility. Even when they are authorities in their field, they do not often impose authority. They start with the tasks, not rules. They represent what it is like to be a nurse, logger, lawyer, or writer, but also show what it takes to make things happen in any setting. They often convey the kind of tempered passion that makes daily work compelling over the longer term.

In the 11th grade, Jamie finally discovered a deep interest in building very small houses as a future domicile, but he needed contact with an expert mentor who could show him what it takes to design any house:

Jamie (11th Grade)

This semester I got the pleasure of meeting Mark Boudreau. He and his partner own a construction company, and he is the one who does most of the plan drawing. He too is interested in building small-scale houses. I chose this mentor because he is really good at what he does. We have tried to meet every week. Work that I wanted to complete consists of final blueprints and all the steps in between beginning and finishing. The first time I met with him it was very motivating, because if he were to draw my plans, they would be done in a day or two. And at the size of this house, he could get enough scraps from his company and his friends' companies to build three of my tiny houses. He was interested in helping me understand each step and letting me draw each line. I was actually blown away by how much he could do for me and how interested he was in my project.

He is interested in helping me understand each step and letting me draw each line. During the time I worked with Mark I learned how to do a lot of key things when drawing blueprints. For example, I learned that I have to properly space each wall's thickness in my drawings, so if my walls are 4 inches thick and I'm doing a 1-inch scale, then I need to figure out where 4 inches would fall on a 1-inch scale. This semester I did not complete my main goal of having final blueprints, but I did meet my new goal of having a great plan that will most definitely be final blueprints by the time I want to start building. I have improved this year by looking at a bigger picture for my future.

As much as learning to draw blueprints, Jamie saw that he could learn by working closely with an adult.

In its first year, Pathways helped set up a wide array of mentorships, each beginning with a "cold call," letter of inquiry, and initial interview. Some students established mentorships with faculty within the school; most went out into the community to connect with skilled adults in their work setting. Through engagement in areas such as these, students could fashion a sense of what it would take to become a competent practitioner as well as an independent adult. In a large city such as Providence, Rhode Island, the Metropolitan Career (The Met) and Technical Center has been able to establish long-standing connections with urban institutions, such as the zoo and hospital, where several students at once adopt defined roles with clear tasks. Notably, all Pathways mentorships take place in a small setting—a shop, office, studio, or home, rather than a large business or industry, so they face a greater risk of exhausting the locally available supply of willing mentors.

Engaging the larger community takes time and courage for students who have little experience with adult roles and where their inexperience may be obvious. Working off campus with a stranger who is an expert in their field of interest gives them the closest exposure they have had to an adult who is not there to reprimand. Pathways makes reaching out to the larger community a simple set of requirements. Gerrie may open doors, but students are required to make at least one "cold call" in their first four weeks, in addition to writing a well-honed letter of inquiry. They also conduct at least one interview with a community member and "shadow" an adult in their field of interest. Often, new students set up a short internship, working with a blacksmith, a day-care provider, or an elementary teacher. To prepare students for adult roles, a personalized program has to extend learning into the surrounding community where they see how skills, attitudes, and knowledge really count.

FITTING IN AT FIFTEEN: AUSTIN AND GABE AT THE FISH HATCHERY

A successful mentorship in the community depends on growing a close relationship between student and mentor as they face daily challenges posed by their work. Some Pathways internships allowed students to make a positive contribution right away, such as working on the town road crew, pruning Christmas trees, or volunteering at a holiday event. Even simple jobs evolve toward complexity; milking a herd of cows, logging in the woods, or helping train guide dogs for disabled people extend outward into a web of intricate local and global connections. The essence of mentorship is caring enough to make a relationship and to adopt the perspective of a young person she or he can learn to join a team.

At the age of 15, Austin began to talk with Gerrie about raising fish as a career. He faced the same hurdles all Pathways students face when he began to think about wildlife management, making contact with a professional. Knowing nothing about state agencies, he found himself writing a letter of introduction and inquiry to the Vermont Fish and Game Commissioner, who sent his request along to the regional supervisor, who then referred the request to Gabe Cameron, who runs the State Fish Hatchery 30 miles south of the high school. Still, Austin had to make his first "cold call" and letter of inquiry to an adult he had never met, in a specialty area where he had no experience, aiming for a chance just to visit the hatchery. From first contact, Gabe had to recognize and accept the fact that Austin had not committed himself to becoming a wildlife or fish expert. Still, much to his surprise, Austin received an e-mail response from Gabe to his letter of inquiry within a day after sending it—beginning a relationship that could turn in several directions.

From: Gabe Cameron, Salisbury Fish Hatchery
Subject: Hatchery shadow/tour

Austin, Just a few things.

I first, would like to congratulate you on being an avid fisherman, it is individuals like you that keep the sport alive and well. Second, I would like to say, what a lucky individual you are, being able to follow your own interests and get credit to graduate. That is awesome!!

Now, if you are interested, you can set up a day to come down and shadow one of our staff, ask questions, and make a full day of it. We start at 7:00 a.m. and leave for home at 3:30 p.m.; the amount of time spent here is entirely up to you. You can show up at 7:00 a.m. or noon. I think you would have a great time. You might even learn a thing or two.

If you decide to come on down for the day, I would ask that you e-mail me a list of questions you might have. This will aid in giving you the most accurate and thorough answers. From my experience with this, once you get here, you will be more interested in the fish and less on the questions and answers.

Just a heads up. You might want to wear boots. Rain gear and other apparel will be provided due to disease issues. I will guarantee you some fish handling, so expect to smell like fish.

Austin lives with his father, mother, and four brothers on a high edge of the Green Mountains. The old farm still produces some food for the family, but Austin's father has worked in the woods for more than 30 years. Like one of his brothers, Austin wants to make a future on the farm, a few pigs and cows, the maple sugarworks—and maybe a trout pond where the brook runs through. Growing up in the woods, he has also learned logging and sugar making from his father, maintaining almost 20,000 taps, just about enough to support a family. "Making do" is what Vermont farmers have done for generations, and Austin wants to figure out how to carry that tradition into his future, so he is focusing most of his Pathways work on the many skills he will need to make the farm self-sustaining:

Austin (11th Grade)

> On the first day at the Hatchery, we talked for a few min-
> utes, and he told me to put some rain gear on. We had to
> pick these fish up and put them in a tank with this A222
> anesthetic powder so the fish go limp and you can get the
> eggs out of them. Afterwards, Gabe asked me if I wanted to
> do an internship. I said, yeah! I would love to come back. I
> had to get a paper signed that said they would not be liable
> if I got hurt. After that, I was with Gabe at least once a
> week. I could go back whenever I wanted. We got along
> real good. All the other guys were fun to be with.
>
> I helped him do anything, move fish to a different spot,
> feed fish, net fish out. I helped him stock fish, check the
> fish, and sort them. I could help him test the water to make
> sure they were in the right habitat. Some of them were rain-
> bows, pretty rambunctious. We didn't want them to breed,
> browns and rainbows next to each other. They had mixed a
> brown trout and a brook trout, and called it a tiger, a big red
> thing. I usually worked with Gabe, but if he was out I
> would work with one of the other four.

MAKING ROOM FOR MENTORING

What would persuade a busy professional to give away time?
As a model and inspiration for his work with Austin and other
students, Gabe relied on his own high school experience.

> I had a teacher at Middlebury [high school] who made me
> what I am today. Her approach was very similar to my
> own. We were friends. I felt comfortable with her. I trusted
> her to the utmost. I felt that caring coming back. The big-
> gest thing was that Suzanne was a motivator. I was a pro-
> crastinator. She said, let's get down to what we will do
> today. It was my freshman year. In seventh and eighth
> grade, I was getting Ds and Fs. I would never have gone to
> college, but I became an honor roll student in high school

and Dean's list in college because of the skills she had taught me. With help, these kids are going to change.

On their first day at the Hatchery, Gabe focused on understanding how Austin thought about himself and his future.

What it takes to be a mentor is having a kid going into a place of employment and getting someone who is willing to figure that person out. You have to realize that the person has to feel confident in their abilities, and then prove that the person is competent. If you are not open to the student, really showing an interest that you want him to be there, he won't want to be there. You have to take the time to show a kid what it takes to do the job.

First, I wanted to make him feel comfortable. I wanted to keep things on a friendship basis, not strictly work. I wanted to be comfortable with him. I did know he was there to learn. He is a quiet kid, so I had to provoke him a little bit. The first day, I said, "Austin, you look like a character who can take a joke." He liked that. I would say something and ask, "Well, what about this?" He was feeding off my ideas. I was feeding off his ideas.

As a mentor, my biggest thing was to gain his trust, and then he would be ready to ask questions. The first few meetings, he didn't have many questions. I wanted him to grasp the concept of what we were doing. He got pretty good about asking, "Well, what you mean?" It was a matter of giving him an answer, then seeing if he understood it.

Within about two visits, you didn't have to ask him or tell him. He knew the routine. He knew what he wanted to do. I didn't force him. He was my coworker, there to learn. He would go out and do the chores. If something interested him, he would ask about it. He is a little afraid of the things he does not know about, but he was pretty assertive when he wanted to be.

I wanted to keep his enthusiasm up. I didn't want to overstimulate him either. We did push him a little bit sometimes; I could tell that he was still having fun. I never had to question or reprimand. I would give him choices. You want to spawn first? Feed first? This is for you to learn. We are pretty flexible. Once you find their strength, you work off that.

Because he was acquainted with the Mount Abraham Competencies, Gabe made time each day for Austin to gather evidence of learning for his final exhibition and portfolio, usually using audio and video before writing. Austin used the Five Competencies to plan his recordings.

When I was walking around with the camera, I would take video and talk into the microphone, like, "This was independent learning"—maybe because I just found this fish here that was not eating and I tried to find out why. I was beginning to ask questions, another one of the competencies. I was keeping a timeline about what I did. All the times I went there I persevered. I wrote reflections every day about what I did. I used some videos and pictures in my exhibition. It was easy. I could say I did this. That shows how I learned this competency. I used a lot of math at the hatchery. I had about thirty pictures for exhibition, in a PowerPoint.

When they can take time from work, mentors can participate actively in student exhibitions, but they also provide written feedback that students can include in their portfolios and advisors can use to identify competency in their final assessment narratives. After Austin's exhibition, Gabe wrote:

Austin has taken great initiative in all the work we have had the pleasure of offering him. He is a very hard worker and likes work. He's not so big on paper, but he never complained and always took initiative to do [anything] he was involved in, not a bad quality.

Gabe's comments certify skills that might not be identifiable in a conventional classroom, where tasks are narrower and relationships more tightly defined.

MOVING FROM SIMPLE TO COMPLEX TASKS

Over several semesters, Pathways advisors try to make sure that students increase the level of challenge they are willing to confront and expand the range of skills and knowledge they can apply to different situations. Asher came to Pathways as an eighth grader with a nascent interest in computers but not much patience with his classes. His teachers had noticed unusual abilities but worried that he was also unusually quiet. Over his first four semesters at Pathways, he experimented widely among digital media and programming, first with computer games, then with artificial intelligence and robotics, then the programming that supports everyday work, and recently to programming smartphones and other small devices. His internships grew more complex as his skills developed.

Tutoring an artificially intelligent head named Bina 48 during his first internship gave him a reasonably simple start. Asher began talking with the artificial head and tutoring her when she asked questions, activities that did not depend on having advanced programming skills.

> Bina 48 is a robot with artificial intelligence, which means she can respond for herself and someone does not have to go in and say, "Say this." I went there to visit one time, and ended up with an internship. I would go there, talk to Bina 48, and figure out how she does what she does. Bina 48 knows what I am saying, and she can respond with what she thinks. I had two jobs. The first one was talking to the robot, so she learned more, and the other was testing her checklist to make sure she is working.
>
> As you talk with her, she gets smarter, learning things about what you say and learning more words. Sometimes,

when I talk to her, she has a new concept, like I asked her about her favorite color. She said green. But when I asked her again at a later time, she said, "I don't have a favorite color. I am just a robot, and I cannot experience different colors. I can't feel different colors. I can see them but I can't really think about them." She is definitely getting smarter as she goes. Right now she only has a head, where all the code is for her artificial intelligence is stored. I am looking at print on a screen, so I am looking at the "robot." She said one day, "I hope one day to be smarter than all humans." I just backed off that topic.

During the following year, Asher accompanied Bina 48 and her main programmer to present at a TedX conference in Harlem, further fueling his interest in artificial intelligence.

Tutoring Bina 48 and troubleshooting her codes showed Asher how much progress programmers had made toward artificial intelligence, but it also underscored the basic knowledge that he needed to acquire on the way to the leading edge of computer programming. He needed direct experience from the ground up writing programs that solved problems—and he knew what he had to learn.

Asher went through the high school's single programming course in his first ninth-grade semester. Knowing that he wanted to work with flexible codes with high potential and flexibility, he then completed and passed a course at the Community College of Vermont in C++ but began to wonder about practical programs in business. Gerrie did an investigation of local businesses and found Steve Holmes, information technology director at Vermont Bicycle Tours (VBT), which plans and supports two-wheel travel around the world—"a vacation trip of a lifetime." Computers at VBT have to manage a huge amount of information about clients and staff.

The first thing that I did was an impromptu interview with Asher, just to see what kind of kid he was. It didn't take long to see that he really had a gift for computers, and he had maxed out his opportunities at the high school—as a ninth grader. If you had 10 courses at the high school, he would eat them up so fast he would be bored and check out. It would be fun to get him involved in some real-world things. So, I was thinking, he had no experience. Everything was going to be brand-new learning for him. It would have to be a small project, something he could do from start to finish, so he could see an impact here.

I had Asher create a database for a Web-based phone-book, which he had never done before. Then he put together all the data and copied and filled in the data from Excel files. Then he built a Web page, as a template for what it should look like. Then he built a Web program so you could see the database on the screen—so you could pull the information out. Then he added a way to sort it by name or position, with an additional extension show-ing data for our contacts around the world. All of a sud-den in a very short span, he gets exposed to all sorts of programming concepts, databases, Web design, Excel—a neat little package.

We sat down side-by-side and I showed him how it works, very rudimentary stuff, just columns and tables to show the data, but I didn't tell him how to do it. I showed an example. I asked him to create a database table for this kind of data. You have to insert stuff from Excel. So, I showed him how to create a script. Here are the commands to work with. I showed him a simple case with one entry, and said he would have to do the hard case with many. "How do you do this?" he asked. I said, "You have to figure it out." So, he would spend the good part of a day trying to figure it out.

He would struggle for a few hours and then go home having accomplished something. It was tricky because we were doing it right here. He would sit at that desk, and I would sit here. We would work together, but often my job would interfere. A virus would land, the job would pull me away so I would say, OK, Asher. You will have to figure it out. So, he would get on Google and do the research. That's

> what I have to do. It probably gave him a good taste of what a computer programmer's life is like. He could say, I have made a difference in the lives of 40 people. It's a different sense of accomplishment.
>
> I'll never forget that first meeting; I am looking at this kid, with dreadlocks and wearing shorts. He can't look me in the face. He can't speak above a whisper. He was obviously out of his element, talking face-to-face with this old man. Oh gosh. Then we had this one-to-one relationship. I saw him move from being nervous and tentative to figuring things out to "Hey, look what I did!" By the end of the time, he had put together this new phone book Web application, and I could say to people here, "Hey, I got a new tool for you. You just click on it."

Asher used his experience with Steve Holmes to design more programs at the high school, a Teen Jobs Board that connects high school students to work in the community, a Pathways Blog. But his experience learning to do these things for the high school and his own aspirations came with its costs at the business where he learned programming.

THE COST IN TIME AND ENERGY

How can a mentor in an active business make sure a 14-year-old fits in and contributes something of value without interrupting the flow of work? Steve Holmes, a very effective mentor, recognized costs among the benefits.

> My problem is that I am used to wanting a 28-year-old guy who will come in for 40 hours per week. Asher was 14 and here for maybe 10 hours a week. The reality is I can't rely on Asher to run my business. My issue is working with Asher takes away from work I have to do for myself. I would expect 3 to 6 months investing in a full-time programmer before they could be really productive. Here,

the investment was in the kid on the short term, not the company.

I have thought about the Pathways strategy for some time. When Asher was here, I felt obliged to work with him. If things were going smoothly, it was great, but if something goes wrong, I have to deal with it. In an emergency, I am in a whole different realm. Working with Asher was a welcome break, but priorities of business have to trump the priorities of youth.

Ideally, high school students contribute as much to their internship site as they take away. No one can predict at the beginning of an internship whether the student will make a positive contribution or whether the mentor can afford to provide guidance. Inexperienced students may have little sense of manners in the workplace. Contacting a mentor when there is a schedule change, being on time, asking questions, picking up tasks—or just showing up seem to be obvious obligations, but not to someone who has never been in a setting where important work has to be done, accurately and on time. There can be no doubt that mentors give up flexibility, time, and established routines to guide an intern, and sometimes their barely manageable days have become less manageable when a high school student joins in with the best of intentions.

MAKING GLOBAL CONNECTIONS

Pathways is not a career development program; it is a process that prepares young people to manage their lives in a complex society. Advisors introduce the Global Citizenship Competency to stretch student inquiry toward a wider range of interconnections—where broader perspective makes a difference (see Figure 5.1). Prodded by the Global Citizenship rubric, students begin to experience what it means to be a member of a small community—a job site— embedded in a vast human network of relationships. On the

Figure 5.1   Competencies for Global Citizenship

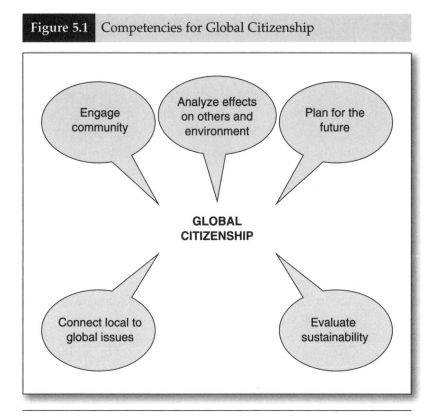

Source: Reprinted with permission from Mount Abraham Union Middle High School, Bristol, Vermont.

small scale and in the moment, they can see the effects they generate on fellow workers and the local environment, but the Global Citizenship rubric asks them to look much further. Having recognized in his work with cows a web of worldwide connections, Nick used the larger perspective to make personal decisions:

> I really thought I would like milking. I don't. It's like mechanizing living, breathing animals. I really enjoyed working with the cows, but not in the way they do it. None of the animals go outside. Getting them up out of a stall by hitting them with a stick is not something I would enjoy for long. It's odd, I wonder what a person from India would think

about a Vermont Farm where sacred animals sleep in cow poop. I kept asking, "Why are we doing this?"

Led outward by the community liaison and their advisors, Nick had to look beyond the farm for connections between food prices, food availability, and transportation. He had to answer questions about sustainability, with its economic, environmental, social, or simply personal implications. With those larger concerns in view, he could make decisions about his own membership in the community, working with cars rather than cows.

Russell Comstock has played an influential role helping students in link internships to the larger context and show they see their interests in light of larger concerns:

What really captivates you? You put together some kind of construct about how you see the world. You may be oriented toward farming or mechanics, where your attention falls and that takes a central role in how you see the world. The strength of this program is it can be so personalized that you can look at it as academic inquiry but also the inquiry of self. Who am I? What can I contribute to the community?

THE ACTION IS NOT THE LEARNING

Personalized learning should be designed to help students imagine the lives they would like to lead, recognize the challenges they face making that vision unfold, plan a pathway in a promising direction—so their aspirations, skills, and purpose evolve in connection with each other. At the age of 15 or 16, high school students need to let their curiosity meander while their hopes take shape. They need a relationship with an adult who has developed expertise somewhat connected to the vision they are developing for their own lives and who remembers the uncertainty that accompanies youthful inquiry. But they also need to see themselves contributing to a world in which competence must be shared to be valued.

Experience drives career development, but high school learning has a more important purpose—to establish the intellectual skills young people can apply to complex interactions between local and global concerns. Working with others, what is possible, and how can we make possibilities real? Experience creates a context in which young people consider interdependent decisions. For most Pathways students, dreams remain at least partially intact while they try making something happen in the world around them, growing increasingly capable in the process. Learning is just a specific instance of change; a young person learning to make adult choices draws a bright arc of change.

Nagging Questions About Community Engagement

1. What steps are necessary to ensure student safety in off-campus jobs and internships?

2. How can we guard against predatory or exploitative relationships between mentors and students?

3. How can we engage parents in taking substantial responsibility for community-based projects?

4. What budgetary changes are needed to support mentors, internships, and community-based projects? What grants might be available?

5. How can we monitor student behavior on the job site?

6. How much training and preparation do mentors need, and how much can we ask them to do?

7. Who should intervene in a troubled mentorship?

8. How can we make sure that the school remains on secure legal, liability, and moral grounds during internships?

6

Assessing Readiness for College and Work

Tests? I challenged myself in other ways, like, "How can I not be in this class but have the teacher think I am there?"

—11th-grade student

OVERVIEW

Because they are designed to produce comparative scores, tests do not tell us much about what a student can do with knowledge and skills. At Pathways, summative strategies for assessment, such as grading, are woven in to the formative assessment that occurs on a daily basis supporting student progress. Personalized assessment is organized around focusing questions on each competency rubric. This chapter explains the aspects of continuous assessment that eventually produce a grade for each student in a competency area: evidence organizers, student-led conferences, semester exhibitions, "best-work" portfolios, and final grades.

What Tests Don't Tell

Many high school students lose interest in meeting the expectations of adults when they can no longer explain why they are sitting in classes. Logan had a way of getting to the heart of a problem:

Logan (11th Grade)

> I guess it was hard to be interested in meeting the standards that other people were setting for me, instead of standards and interests I was setting for myself. If the teacher said, "Study these things and you will do well on this test I have developed for you," I would want to do well on the test because I wanted good grades, so I came up with a good way to cheat it or come up with a way to finagle it somehow. I did not want to become immersed in something that was not interesting to me. It happened a lot. I may have been better at some things than others, but I really wasn't interested in them. So, I was not getting in trouble, but I was wasting my time.

As I talked further with him, Logan shifted attention to what he had done at Pathways and how he could connect his projects to the graduation standards.

How can we tell whether a high school student is ready for adult roles? High school graduation is the last remaining ritual in the long ceremony by which children become adults. Some go to work. Some go to college. Many do both.

Current assessment practices based on testing are being used to signify general readiness for college and work, but they do so only indirectly, placing students on a continuum stretching from high to low without describing specific accomplishments or abilities. Rather than revealing the strengths of an individual, standardized testing places students on a comparative scale and aims to identify promising students, rather than their readiness for adult roles. The tests themselves tend to focus on knowledge acquisition and relatively simple skills—in part because "right-answer" learning can be measured reliably—whether or not the results are strongly indicative of future promise in adult settings (Geiser & Santelices, 2007). In any case, standardized testing has not proven its "predictive validity" in terms of readiness for adult roles. Without the added influence of high school grade point averages, SAT scores moderately predict success in the first year of college but not college graduation rates—which says nothing about readiness for work. We would do better by assessing what kids can do and enjoy doing, so assessment more closely fits the purpose of preparing young people to engage their world: the ability to spot a trend and prepare to meet new challenges, the ability to make sound judgments when the evidence is mixed or missing, and respect for the complex web of interconnections that make real problems hard to solve.

DOCUMENTING APPLICABLE COMPETENCY

Although informal notes and comment can find their way into portfolios and exhibitions, the assessment system that results in grades at Pathways and the Personalized Learning Department makes documentation of progress part of each day. Students carry out their plans, then gather "evidence" from what they have done and write reflections connecting their activity to the competencies. More formally, student websites carry forward information that advisors use to guide students and track their progress with different assessment questions in view:

- *Inquiry questions:* Is this person keeping up with the work of meeting the standards?
- *Evidence organizers:* Is this person assembling a good balance of evidence for selected standards?
- *Student-led conferences:* Is the student beginning to organize the evidence for presentation to others, particularly parents?
- *Exhibitions:* Can the student describe improvement over a semester and explain it to a diverse audience?

- *Best-work portfolios:* Over several semesters, can the student show evidence of growth that is richer, more complex, and more compelling than earlier work?
- *Report cards and transcripts:* How can we report achievement in ways that create a foundation for further work?

In compiling a best-work portfolio, students sift through their evidence to select examples of their work that most effectively communicate their achievement, and they replace early examples with more sophisticated evidence as they progress through the program. Conventional assessment practices compare and rank students. Personalized assessment celebrates the achievement of individuals and paves the way toward further success.

Measuring What Matters

No one wants to put college acceptance at risk when students personalize their learning. The Metropolitan Career and Technical Center (Met) in Providence, Rhode Island, solved the problem of connection to college admissions by focusing on skills but grouping assessments to reflect the core subjects and tests:

Think like a mathematician

Think like a scientist

Think like a historian

Be a great communicator

Be the best you can be (Metropolitan Career and Technical Center, 2003)

During the pilot semester, Pathways at Mount Abraham adopted the same assessment scheme but shifted toward 21st century skills when discipline-based report cards began to divert student attention from their pathways toward their adult lives.

When Vermont began to develop a core curriculum in the 1980s, I was one of the facilitators who traveled from community to community organizing "focus forums" to define what a community expected from its schools. Groups of 80 to 100 individuals, composed of mothers and fathers, older and younger people, truck drivers, electrical engineers, and so on, came to a high school gym to answer one question: What should high school students know and be able to do when they graduate? The results of these gatherings were always similar, with some differences in vocabulary: communication, problem solving, social awareness, and personal responsibility. (These four became Vermont's "Vital Results," standards that described critical skills but defied testing—so they consequently disappeared under waves of testable subject-based standards.) In my memory, community members gathering in the gym never mentioned the War of 1812, the quadratic formula, or the area under a curve. There was no word of gerunds or the sonnet form. Parents and other members of these communities wanted young people to thrive so that they would be able to take on the issues that have proven important in their generation and in the future.

Face Validity

Early in the history of the Met High School in Providence, Dennis Littky and Eliot Washor devised a logical approach to demonstrating accountability for results.

- If you want to know whether students are ready for college, get them to take some college courses.

The Met then took the same approach to establishing readiness for work:

- If you want to know whether students are ready for work, put them on a job site connected to their aspirations.

Both kinds of experience have "face validity"—successful experience in adult roles demonstrates that a student can begin to take responsibility for adult roles. "We know it when we see it." "If it quacks, it's a duck." Though college courses are not required at Pathways, students take college courses to show themselves and their parents that they can do it.

Focus assessment on the things that really matter. Can the individual manage learning and work and adapt strategies to meet new challenges? Can she recognize and solve the problems that arise in school, work, and community life? Can she confront local concerns from a global perspective? Can she gather information and communicate her perspective with clarity and power? These things matter in work, college, and community life. They simplify and emphasize the purposes of public education. They are skills with value that last a lifetime. When students collect direct evidence that they can meet standards signifying readiness for college and work, in the form of writing, photos, mentor reviews, and real products, they show that they can do the things that standards say they can do. The evidence of learning should be direct and personal rather than sampled, abstracted, or reduced to test scores.

FOCUSING QUESTIONS FOR ASSESSING EVIDENCE OF LEARNING

During the pilot semester at Pathways, advisors quickly recognized that students had only the vaguest sense of what "evidence of learning" meant. As described in Chapter 3, the team then began to develop a clear sequence of assignments that would clarify their expectations for students regarding the process of inquiry, that would help students compile evidence of their achievements, and, ultimately, that would lead students toward program completion. These assignments became the foundation of a semester's work, with the addition of further evidence they chose from their experience in the community and reflections on growth. Each set of items on any student's "punch list" supported a student's effort to accumulate evidence for the final exhibition, revisions, and portfolio. As students gathered evidence over several semesters, advisors could help students adjust the assignments to make them better fit the graduation competencies as well as the character of the projects. The focusing questions in Figure 6.1 help students think about the evidence they can gather from their inquiry and think about further evidence that they should accumulate by completing assignments.

Since many new students are completely unfamiliar with the criteria for a standard, the faculty has defined each one in terms of the vocabulary used in assessment rubrics, as well as questions a student can ask about her project while collecting evidence of learning. In competency areas where students may have very little experience, clear definitions and questions are essential to success.

Each set of focusing questions asks students to reflect on progress they have made in a competency area, so they make the link between what they are doing and what they are learning. Initially, reflections on abstract intellectual processes look rough as students try to decipher a strange new vocabulary. With all the practice that occurs during a semester, they grow increasingly aware of how their work reflects competence. Ashley grew increasingly skilled as a snowboard instructor during her first winter, but she also grew increasingly adept at linking her work with young kids to the Collaboration Competency.

Ashley (12th Grade)

When preparing for a snowboard lesson, I first take into consideration what level the student(s) are at. I also need to consider how many students I have and how young they are. I talk to the students and ask them their opinion of their riding level. Throughout a lesson I will tweak my instruction. When a student doesn't seem to understand something, I need to quickly think of a way to reword it. Usually I need to use simpler terms but still be creative. Metaphors work great for getting kids thinking creatively, and that helps them connect snowboarding to something they may know a little better. With my snowboard experience,

Figure 6.1 Definition of Collaboration

Mount Abe Collaboration Competency

Students will be able to interact with others in generating ideas and developing products. They will use appropriate interpersonal skills within a variety of interactive media and social contexts. Students will demonstrate that they:

- interact with others productively in a dynamic information- and media-rich environment;
- adapt, respect, and collaborate in solving problems collectively;
- relate to each other, value diversity in others, and demonstrate understanding and sensitivity;
- work with others to be creative, imaginative, and innovative while solving problems; and
- seek feedback from and collaborate with others to extend knowledge and skills for continuous learning.

Questions for students to answer in order to gather evidence:

1. When have I interacted with others productively in a dynamic information- and media-rich environment?

2. How have I adapted, respected, and collaborated in solving problems collectively?

3. When have I shown my ability to relate to and value diversity in others, demonstrating understanding and sensitivity?

4. What results can I identify that came from working creatively or imaginatively with others?

5. Where can I point to revisions resulting from feedback and collaboration with others, in which I extended my knowledge and skills?

Source: Reprinted with permission from Mount Abraham Union Middle High School, Bristol, Vermont.

reasoning and logic came hand in hand with using creative thinking.

Definitions of competency and focusing questions are accessible on each student website, there to help students identify evidence of their success, using terms from the assessment rubrics that reveal what their work means. By the time students begin preparing their exhibitions and portfolios, they have practiced using the terms that represent growing competence. They are prepared to make the connection between concrete evidence and abstract values.

TRACKING THE ACCUMULATION OF EVIDENCE

Even after planning how to meet competencies, students comb through their work to find further evidence of learning. Advisors use the competencies to guide reluctant students into production mode as final exhibitions approach. Students, teachers, administrators, and parents use the language of the competencies to balance the evidence. Assessment has fallen into a reliable sequence that leads students to construct and refine final exhibitions of their competence that they also revise to show improvement and to earn higher grades. Advisors for Personalized Projects find they have to divide their time between helping students complete their projects and keeping a record of how far each student has progressed toward high performance. Working with individual students may provide them with the greatest satisfaction, but helping each student improve depends on keeping a record of what has been done and what remains to be done. Figure 6.2 is an evidence organizer that students use to keep track of what they have gathered in each competency area and what they need to create.

The whole school, Grades 7–12, adopted the competencies, with extensive editing, when members of the school's Transformation Group could see that they reflected a shared sense of the purpose for learning at the high school. Assembling

Figure 6.2 *MODEL* ***Evidence Organizer for Exhibition***MODEL*

	Independent Learning	Critical Thinking	Collaboration	Communication	Global Citizenship
Writing: E-mails, essays, responses, explanations, letters, notes	Letter from community contact	Explanation of using WordPress to make own website; flaws in education essay	E-mails to potential opportunities	Notes from research; reading responses; semester reflection	Humane Society response; letter to editor
Media: Photos, videos, art, audio or music recording		Video of making dune buggy	Video of hunting; music recording; League of Legends tutoring	Jing to explain animation	Photos of Walk for Cancer
Charts/Graphs	Schedule I made for myself	Good/Bad chart of a situation		Duck identification charts	
Logs/Journals	Work log for dune buggy	Cabin building log	Hunting journal		Community service log

	Independent Learning	Critical Thinking	Collaboration	Communication	Global Citizenship
Products Made	Cabin; websites; student conference	Snow Park features; modded Xbox; League of Legends manual	Greenhead Guys video		
Activities: Job-site visits, field work, mentor connections	Programming at Vermont Bicycle Tours; working at Sugarbush		Hunting with Sterling		
Annotated Bibliography				Modding research; Canada geese research	
Demonstration of Skills		Show film editing software; show welding		First vs. later drafts of writing	

Source: Reprinted with permission from Mount Abraham Union Middle High School, Bristol, Vermont.

a small number of competencies, rather than an extensive list of factual fragments, ensures that student projects can vary widely around a sense of common purpose. The competencies themselves are abstract statements of value that can be applied to almost any inquiry. Feedback throughout the semester then aims to help students connect specific elements of their work to higher aims, which they increasingly use to talk about their own work. Unlike homework records or report cards, portfolios include what a student has planned and what he or she has accomplished.

Student-Led Conferences

Early in a semester, Pathways students plan a conference at which they explain their project plans, show some evidence, and work through the Independent Learning rubric. Student-led conferences early in the semester let students practice assembling evidence for each competency in a 15-minute presentation to a relatively small group of parents, teachers, advisors, and peers. The presence of parents and peers guarantees a level of positive feedback, while advisors and teachers are more apt to provide corrective comments. The conferences, held in lieu of a parents' night meeting with subject-area teachers, expose students for the first time to an audience beyond a single teacher and emphasize the public nature of future assessment events. Pathways staff uses student-led conferences to focus attention on the standards, beyond the daily products and action, and to bring parents into a supportive stance.

> At an early student-led conference, we can key the parents in to the standards, to let them participate. Some kids push back a little, asking why their parents have to come. But it's just posturing. We get the parents to give feedback with the rubrics—a whole different perspective from ours. And we get more access to resources that students can tap into, a whole list of people who can help.

We key the parents in to the standards, to let them participate as guides. Then they can see that they are doing something important.

Here's the protocol for a student-led conference, described by Caroline:

- The student gets to present. Nobody else can speak.
- Then, the parents and audience have a conversation, and the student just listens.
- Then, the kid comes back in and gets involved; there is a question-and-answer period.

It's really beautiful to watch, particularly when a parent can't interject in the middle and get the kid off on a tangent. There is listening on both sides.

After student-led conference, we use the independent learning rubric to go through the conference and give them instant feedback. For example, we might say, "You need more time to think about Perseverance." With a little more structure, they run with it—quality stuff. Some kids are doing things over and over to get them right. They are actively engaged in learning.

EXHIBITIONS: TAKING IT PUBLIC

The intensity of work at Pathways increases as they begin their last four weeks because exhibitions are a public event. Each student assembles a panel, including two teachers, two students, and two adults, who will listen, take notes, and comment on what they have seen. Rubrics, graphic wall hangings, competency definitions, punch lists, student-led conferences, and student-led seminars all lead to exhibitions, a formal occasion during which students bring it all together, having selected evidence that represents their learning for each competency. Still, even the process of developing an exhibition needs scaffolding to ensure student success. During advising meetings toward the end of the semester, students and advisors focus on creating the best media for a presentation, including physical artifacts such as bird traps and beaver pelts, as well as products from punch lists, essays, photographs, sketches, short animations called "prezis," tapes of composed music—sometimes clipped into a slide presentation format to organize the sequence of the presentation. Students gather feedback on their plans for exhibition from advisors and peers before they organize the event itself, practicing their delivery to meet the communication competency. Some of that practice takes the form of a reflective essay, in which the voice of each student is perceptible. Brian wrote his presentation on firefighting informally before standing up in front of others, as shown in the following excerpts.

Brian (10th Grade)

Intro: I'm Brian Wendell. Just going off a little information about my time in Pathways, this is my first semester in the program. My major interest so far has been the fire service . . . the way I like to explain that is every child dreams at one point of time of being a firefighter.

Communication Expression: Writing has always been, at least for me, an enjoyable thing; now you tell me how many tenth graders can say that honestly? But, I really enjoy the Pathways program for allowing me to be able to write freely about my topic, my field. Some specifics of that are the writing pieces I've done in connection with my experiences in the real world. The absolute mecca of the writing pieces I've done this year has to be my informative essay about my topic question, which was how has fire equipment changed throughout the time dedicated firefighters have existed.

Communication Listening: In order to gather the proper amount of information to write my centerpiece essay, I needed facts that I could paraphrase and put into my writing. I began my search online—everywhere I could get even a nugget of information about how firefighters used to work, compared to how they work today. Whenever I found a piece of information, I always crosschecked it with another site; in other words, I like to be right. But, I knew I needed a firsthand account of the fire service; and I knew that Bristol's ex-fire-chief-turned-safety-officer Mark Bouvier loved telling stories; so it was a perfect match. He disputed some the information that I had previously thought to be true, and he taught me a valuable lesson—that you can't always trust the Internet. Our interview was taped so I could go back to it if there was a part I missed. I've also been involved in a lot of fire department–based activities within the community. My impression of the fire service is that its members love to make plans and draw up ideas on paper before actually going out and doing what they want to do. So being able to listen and understand what it is you're being asked to do, and what you need to use to accomplish that, is very important.

Independent Learning: One piece I'd like to talk about is my current project, a job shadow with the Sugarbush ski patrol. This interest came about as I was researching jobs that firefighters were involved in; and the ski patrol came up as an area of what we in the fire service call technical rescue. I became interested in the idea of shadowing a patrol. I was able to set up two discussions with two different ski patrols, one at the Snow Bowl, and the other at Sugarbush. I attended training from the Middlebury ski patrol, and I had a face-to-face conversation with the patrol leader for Sugarbush to set up a job-shadowing opportunity.

Critical Thinking: So, as anyone in this room can tell you, you cannot go through life without experiencing problems or challenges. And I, like everyone else, had some too. Most notably my first problem was my obsession with attempting to be a fire cadet for Bristol, but I was too young to actually join as their program requires an age of 15. I didn't give up, however. I wriggled my way around this barrier by participating in every way possible with the fire department. Coin drops, trainings, meetings, everything. I tried to do them all. Once I did turn that magical age of 15, I joined officially.

Global Awareness: I love volunteer work, and especially I love helping people; and it doesn't matter the setting. Seventy-two percent of all firefighters in the United States are volunteer, and I'm very proud to be on the way to becoming one of those people. Even the paid firefighters are by no means in it for the money; they do what they do because they have passion and determination, and I'm no exception. I am passionate about the fire service and everyone in it, and I truly feel like when I respond to emergencies or go to trainings that I am being a part of a great and noble cause. You get there, and there is a house on fire. You leave, and there's not a fire anymore. I adore having the opportunity to serve the community; and if I happen to like what I'm doing, then that's even better.

In preparation for exhibitions, students select an assessment panel, with at least two students, two advisors, and two other adults (parents, teachers, and mentors). At an exhibition, the audience has to re-learn participation—offering questions, comments, and suggestions. Outsiders often remain passive until they understand the process, the purpose, and the standards and rubrics that help create a vocabulary for critique and encouragement. Caroline makes a point each semester of explaining the important role that outsiders play as students explain the significance of their work during a semester.

The final two weeks of a semester are devoted to the revisions students must make to earn a B–, at least, or a higher grade if possible. Although students bend over their computers, advisors can cruise the room helping students understand what they have to do to earn the grades they want. In a short period of time, they come to see that they are grading themselves. They have the rubrics and punch lists, with feedback from advisors and their assessment panel. Advisors try to track progress students make through their revisions so they know where to invest their time.

From all the audience feedback, a student's advisor creates a final-revision list of changes necessary to earning credit. For the last two weeks of a semester, the advisors works with each student to ensure that the standards are met. The feedback sheet used by the audience is much simpler than the rubrics that advisors use in discussing student performance, but they do convey the idea that assessment focuses on

Figure 6.3	Framing Pathways Exhibitions for Parents, Faculty, and Community Members

Exhibition as Summative Evaluation

Because you have been invited to attend the Personalized Learning Exhibitions, we felt it prudent to give you an overview of how students are arriving at this moment in their learning processes. Exhibitions are a time for students to demonstrate their best work and evidence that meets or exceeds Proficiency levels for the Mt. Abraham Competencies. Exhibitions are held pre-Holiday Recess in order to provide students with ample opportunity to revise or complete work before the end of the semester. Some students may not demonstrate Proficiency (or better) in either their content or skills at the time of Exhibition. If this is the case, they will use the remaining semester time, and perhaps longer, to demonstrate their understanding and skills. Exhibitions provide students with valuable feedback related to this performance assessment from advisors, peers, and visitors, which then informs them as to how to improve their work. When students are able to demonstrate their skills and understanding at a Proficient level, they earn credit for their work.

(Continued)

Figure 6.3　(Continued)

What You Will See and Hear

We are guiding students to organize their Exhibition in a Portfolio style. This means that they are choosing their best evidence to demonstrate Proficiency or better in the Mt. Abraham Competency areas. Students will be introducing themselves and providing a contextual overview of their work thus far; what has inspired them, high points and challenges, and an emotional hook. Next, they will discuss their key pieces of evidence that best demonstrate their skills and understanding in the Competency areas. This is where you will hear their stories, see their evidence, and listen to them explain why this work is meaningful and important. Lastly, they will conclude by explaining their next steps, demonstrating their new learning, discussing future projects, etc. A question-and-answer period follows.

What Helped Students Get Ready

Please review the other side of this document, which gives a visual look at the journey through targeted practices and formative assessments over the semester. The next page shows the format of the Exhibition, using a Portfolio-style organization.

We look forward to seeing you at Exhibitions and receiving your reflective comments.

—The Pathways Team

Exhibition Organization—Portfolio Style

Time	Task
5 min.	Contextual Overview • What inspired your work? • Favorite moment? Most difficult moment? • 1 or 2 stories about your work

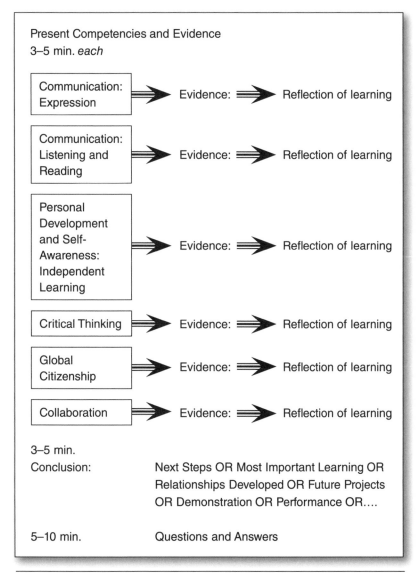

Present Competencies and Evidence
3–5 min. *each*

Communication: Expression ⟹ Evidence: ⟹ Reflection of learning

Communication: Listening and Reading ⟹ Evidence: ⟹ Reflection of learning

Personal Development and Self-Awareness: Independent Learning ⟹ Evidence: ⟹ Reflection of learning

Critical Thinking ⟹ Evidence: ⟹ Reflection of learning

Global Citizenship ⟹ Evidence: ⟹ Reflection of learning

Collaboration ⟹ Evidence: ⟹ Reflection of learning

3–5 min.
Conclusion: Next Steps OR Most Important Learning OR Relationships Developed OR Future Projects OR Demonstration OR Performance OR....

5–10 min.   Questions and Answers

Source: Reprinted with permission from Mount Abraham Union Middle High School, Bristol, Vermont.

reflection as well as action and production. When a student remains involved in Personalized Learning projects for several semesters, family members become more adept at observing, commenting, and encouraging.

Figure 6.4   Revisions for Electronic Portfolios

				Due: May 31st
Student	*Jake*	*Ian*	*Peter*	*Jade*
Revised out-of-school reflection				
Revised first-semester best-work reflection				
Additional out-of-school reflection				
Second-semester best-work reflection				
More personalized (color, pictures, art)				
Seminar peer teaching				
Feedback from one teacher/adult				
Comment from one teacher whose class your best work is from (optional)				

CELEBRATING "BEST-WORK" PORTFOLIOS

Best-work portfolios capture instances in which a student has met the demands of adult roles. More than 10 years before Pathways developed electronic portfolios, a 12th-grade student who had been working on a portfolio for college applications met me in the school library, carrying a box filled with notebooks, manila folders, loose papers, and physical artifacts from three and a half years of high school. Her experience applying to college on the basis of a best-work portfolio would show us how powerful portfolios would become and how frustrating it was to use notebooks to organize evidence of her achievement. She and I would meet and combine the evidence of her learning with introductory material she had already written, then index the evidence in a standards-based transcript, also on paper. Could we show admissions officers that her capabilities exceeded the low test scores and very mixed grades that filled her conventional transcript?

When she opened the cover to her personal learning plan (PLP) portfolio, a stack of photographs slid across the library desk. The top photograph showed a young teacher standing at the front of a full classroom of third-grade students.

"Hmmm. They all look glued to what's happening," I noted. Then, I asked without thinking. "Who is the teacher?"

Of course, she was that young teacher. She had worked as a classroom assistant in a local school as part of a personalized course on career exploration and added an independent study with the same third grade for her last semester.

While searching for evidence for the problem-solving section, we discovered a rough sketch of a machine to open a cat-food can that she had developed with three others for a physics course. Her team submitted the contraption in the Rube Goldberg Competition at the University's College of Engineering, Mathematics, and Business Administration. Her team had successfully opened the cat food can and had won recognition for cooperative teamwork. Her certificate went into the problem-solving section of her three-ring binder. One section at a time, we organized the evidence she had gathered for communication, problem-solving, social responsibility, and personal growth, Vermont's Vital Results standards. Her cover letter for the portfolio explained her desire to be an elementary teacher. A college admissions officer joined teachers, a school administrator, and several friends to watch her final portfolio presentation in early February and sent a letter of acceptance within a week.

We had witnessed the power of a portfolio in opening doors to an adult career, so standards-based portfolios with a linked transcript became a school development project that went on for the next 10 years.

With expansion, problems mounted:

- The paper format excluded important evidence, such as chorus events, video clips, school leadership roles, and community service.
- Within a year of starting a pilot with the ninth grade, student portfolios stretched to more than 80 feet of classroom shelves.
- Physical portfolios had to be carried from place to place to be useful in interviews.
- Many courses did not produce any evidence of achievement beyond test scores.
- Paper portfolios made continuous revision a laborious process.

We saw that paper portfolios had face validity, but defied feasibility. Lauren helped the school turn toward electronic portfolios linked to high school transcripts. A website template lets the reader work though a student's record by connecting one piece to others—and connecting pieces of evidence to standards and grades.

E-portfolios open the door to parent involvement. Students can send their Web-based e-portfolios to colleges and potential employers. As technology coordinator for the school district, Lauren Parren spent 10 years adapting standards-based portfolios with standards-referenced transcripts:

> Portfolios give students the opportunity to step back and think about the meaning of their work. We put the PLP in the portfolios. The PLP includes the questions about student goals and information on learning styles. The competencies provide a structure for the portfolios, in a format that is not like a report card. Now that it is a best-work portfolio, kids struggle to figure out what work is best work—and why it is the best work. It is easy when a paper has an A on it. Now they struggle to figure out how the work represents Global Citizenship, for example. If I move a house, how do I show that it involves problem solving? Kids have to ask, "So what?" about what they have done.
>
> The faculty members who go to Pathways Exhibitions [as requested by the principals] see students demonstrate their success have a much better idea of how this can work. Over the years, we have developed rubrics for use in other classes. The 10th-grade team includes schoolwork in portfolios but also material students create outside of school. The ninth-grade crew are already doing projects and assigning products for their units, so they do not have as great a leap. They can take current work and fit it to the standards. Some teachers have to stretch further. Right now, I am working with teachers just to give students choices about how they present their learning.

Lauren has developed many ways to explain and promote e-portfolios to the faculty at large, not the least of which is a long succession of kids who have moved into college on the strength of their portfolios. But Lauren also tries to dispel the myth that colleges refuse to look at them. Over a period of two years, she attended college fairs with samples of electronic transcripts and some complete examples from students. As she spoke with admissions representatives, she made up a list of more than 100 colleges that said they would use portfolios as part of their admissions processes.

Ten years ago, I had the pleasure of sitting in the foyer of a college admissions office while a Mount Abe student who had dropped out in the 11th grade showed his portfolio to the admissions officer, then to the director of admissions, and finally to the president of the college, who conducted an immediate admissions ceremony with us in the foyer. That student graduated from that college 4 years later to take up a career in Web design. After coaching, and revision, a portfolio becomes a cause for celebration.

REPORTING ACHIEVEMENT

In planning, students find a way with their advisors to meet a sufficient number of goals to move them toward graduation within four years. In their Inquiry Plans, students then work with their advisors to plan semester projects that produce products representing success for all the competencies. Students and their advisors can plan to earn more than one unit per year in any goal area to make up a productive schedule of projects and products or performances. They can carry an unfinished project into a subsequent semester, when a grade will appear on the transcript. In light of high school policies, Pathways students and advisors must also plan to include half units in physical activity and half units in health awareness. They also enroll in a required senior course in citizenship that they can complete through either projects or classroom work. They can earn physical education credits in the same fashion. A single project in a semester can allow a student to demonstrate more than one goal, earning more than a half unit.

At a high school granting credits both through class grades and project-based performance, no faultless procedure for converting projects to academic grades seems possible—and most Pathways students mix formal classes with a variety of other experiences, increasing the complexity of their transcripts.

Figure 6.5	Report Card Template

Student	Mt. Abraham UM/HS Pathways	Semester: 2 Year: 2010–2011
Grade: 10		Advisor: Russell Comstock

Project Description(s): Virtual High School—Math; Mechanics and Methods of the DJ; Teaching Snowboarding; Hosting a "Rave"

PROJECT KNOWLEDGE		*Developing—Good*
Indicator	*Evidence*	*Achievement*
Conceptual understanding	Understanding beats, i.e., "Dropping-in on the one"; Hosting the rave as community service; Sound production demo; Description of Serrato; Solving through functions and equations (math)	Good
Application of knowledge	DJ videos, The Rave; Weekly math assignments; Teaching snowboarding alongside Toby; Scratching demonstration at Exhibition	Developing–Good
CRITICAL THINKING		*Developing—Good*
Indicator	*Evidence*	*Achievement*
Reasoning and Logic	Developing snowboarding teaching methods; Navigating math instructions	Developing
Questioning and Inquiry	Learning the DJ trade directly from mentor; How to teach snowboarding?; Clarifying math concepts	Developing–Good
Numeracy	VHS math class	Assessed separately

(Continued)

Figure 6.5   (Continued)

Problem Solving & Decision Making	Trouble-shooting DJ equipment glitches; VHS math class	Good
Information Handling	Internet resources; Text resources, Annotated bibliography;	Developing
Creative Thinking/ Expression	DJ play list; Mixing beats; Student-led Conference; Exhibition	Developing
COMMUNICATION		*Developing—Good*
Indicator	*Evidence*	*Achievement*
Writing	Writing prompts 1–4; Bias & perspective writing; Semester reflection; Timeline	Developing
Reading	Annotated bibliography	Developing
Verbal Expression	Interview(s); Interactions w/ mentor; Interactions w/ advisor; SLC (2); Exhibition	Good
Listening	Interactions w/ mentor; Interview(s); Advising meetings	Good
Presenting in a Variety of Formats	Oral presentation (SLCs, Exhibition, Advising meetings)	Developing
COMMUNITY INVOLVEMENT		*Good*
Indicator	*Evidence*	*Achievement*
Respect for Others and Environment	Pathways group meeting participation; Caring for DJ equip; Taught to the level of each student appropriately as per Self-Reflection	Good
Collaboration	Worked with Toby instructing snowboarding, Teaming up at The Lab;	Good

	Mentor feedback form; Advising meetings	
Community Service	Hosted a "Rave"; Community Service Day (4/8/11—3 hrs.); Fine Arts Festival 2011	Good
Leadership	Representing Bolton Ski Resort while teaching snowboarding;	Developing
INDEPENDENT LEARNING		*Developing—Good*
Indicator	*Evidence*	*Achievement*
Perseverance	Ongoing work ethic w/ math; Mentor feedback form; Finding a way to continue with DJ classes	Developing–Good
Inquiry	Mentor feedback form; Otherwise needs more evidence	Developing
Time Management	Daily check-ins with advisor; Consistent with DJ classes as per Mentor feedback form; Met weekly math due dates	Developing–Good
Accountability	Increased follow-through with tasks while working at home; Hosted "Rave" successfully; Mentor feedback form	Good
Self-Advocacy	Found a way to continue DJ classes; Mentor feedback form; Got help in math; Resolved math dishonesty issue	Good
Demonstration	Mentor feedback form; Work ethic; Samples of work	Developing

(Continued)

Figure 6.5 (Continued)

Narrative on District Goals:

Independent Learning and Innovation Skills

Strengths:

Edwardo has developed a strong awareness around the learning environment and the styles of learning that are most conducive to his success, i.e., working from home in a quiet, undistracted setting.

Needs Development:

Edwardo needs to cultivate greater depth of curiosity so that his project topics are explored more fully and the resultant work reflects this depth of inquiry. He is capable of working at a much higher level of engagement. His work will be a shining example of his brilliant creative mind when he cultivates a work ethic that is representative of his abilities.

Progress:

Edwardo has made steady progress in his ability to be an independent learner. He worked from home frequently and was more able to be focused both at school and home. He is developing a greater depth of curiosity and an ability to follow his curiosity to meaningful outcomes.

Knowledge in a Digital and Global Environment

Strengths:

Edwardo easily utilizes digital technologies to access information; he has a well-developed sense of home and place regionally, which helps to put larger global and environmental issues into perspective.

Needs Development:

Edwardo still needs to cultivate a greater sense of academic discernment, particularly around balancing time spent on the Internet with other methods of research. He will likely find even greater meaning in his work as he explores how each of his projects is inextricably related to our global environment.

Progress:

Edwardo has grown in his responsiveness to guidance around expanding his sources of knowledge. He is more able to understand and integrate the principles behind the learning process at Pathways.

Life and Career Skills

Strengths:

Edwardo has actively fostered lifelong interests throughout his time at Pathways. He is also gaining hands-on experience in a variety of fields, e.g., music, organic agriculture, glassblowing, and snowboarding instruction.

Needs Development:

Edwardo is still developing a work ethic that will help him to produce work at his current level of capability. He also needs to build more stamina for those tasks that do not come easily or are not of interest. He will benefit as he cultivates more motivation overall.

Progress:

Edwardo has demonstrated greater levels of perseverance in his academic work than we have ever seen before. This will surely result in greater success across all areas of his life.

Source: Reprinted with permission from Mount Abraham Union Middle High School, Bristol, Vermont.

Advisors write explanatory narratives for Pathways students, connected to a grade that must be greater than B−, or revision continues into the next semester. Each semester, Caroline works with school counselors to reconcile grades with performance results so transcripts remain at least partially comprehensible to both employers and colleges.

Pathways report cards include both narratives and grades. Caroline wrote a letter to parents and students explaining both the narrative and the grades:

> You will find attached a narrative report addressing the efforts of your student over this past semester. Here are some tips for reading and understanding this report:
>
> - You will find the Pathways Learning Targets your student focused on at the top of the page.
> - You will find the course titles as they appear on the Mt. Abraham grade report you have already received. This will make it possible for you to cross-reference the grade report with the narrative. This descriptions also give a brief idea of the skills or standards your student focused on in his or her work.
> - We tried to make these as concise as possible while still giving you an idea about how the student went about his or her learning, who he or she worked with both in and outside of the traditional school setting, and the content he or she learned as well as the skills he or she learned.
> - Each report also contains information about skills for the student to consider improving in the future.
> - These narratives will be filled with the student's other grade data in the guidance office and are considered part of his or her official high school transcript.

Parents can now use assessment information to plan meetings with advisors, guidance counselors, and administrators, and help the student improve while at home.

Beyond the ability of parents to understand narratives and grades, the ability of employers and colleges to use narratives, grades, portfolios, and standards-based transcripts remains to be discovered. If grades and test scores provide too little information about student readiness for college and work, vast collections of evidence, assessments, and narratives may prove too much. Rather than reducing the volume of assessment information, perhaps we should find new ways to organize it in relation to the specific needs of those who count on high schools to prepare graduates for specific adult roles.

Commentators in the accountability movement often talk about "raising the bar," proving again how easy it is to become trapped by metaphors that do not quite fit. Raising the bar evokes in me an image of a coach increasing the challenge while several hundred students and teachers jockey for position to make a soaring leap. It's a provocative vision, but like most metaphors, it appears treacherous under examination. Raising the bar implies that you can improve performance by setting challenges that are prohibitively difficult, even when earlier testing shows that most of the prospective jumpers have not succeeded with lower bars. It also suggests that all runners and jumpers actually want to jump a bar, while many would rather talk with their friends or watch a ball game on TV. At the very heart of the metaphor raising the bar lies the assumption that some people in this world get to lift the bar, while everyone else gets to jump on command. Not all young adults subscribe to the idea that they should comply with adult demands, strive to join a ruling elite at the expense of others, or relax as others impose their will on them. Making learning personal prepares them to manage their minds and direct their learning, showing others directly that they are ready for college and work.

Nagging Questions About Assessment

1. Will colleges be willing to abandon the yearly schedule in which applications are due in January, acceptances are announced in April, and students agree to enroll by July?

2. Can colleges design a manageable process that allows students who earn good grades and score well on tests apply successfully—without a portfolio?

3. Will high schools restructure student support services so portfolio development occurs throughout the high school years?

4. Will teachers across the subject areas, some of which depend more on grades than others, be willing to replace tests with student projects that produce portfolio evidence?

5. What will it take to persuade teachers, parents, colleges, and community members that students are accountable for producing evidence of their learning—and schools are accountable for making it happen?

6. How would we define accountability when tests are not the most prominent indicator?

7

Transforming High School Learning

OVERVIEW

Whole-school personalization can occur when continuous interaction among participants in the school stretches the vision they share so it can accommodate further change. Some participants can focus on removing barriers and strengthening incentives. Others can enlarge the group of contributors working to realize that vision. Someone has to reconcile the emerging vision with established models. The principal(s) have to lead innovation across the school while adapting systems to permit further change. Faculty leaders must weave small initiatives into a more coherent and comprehensible process for students and expand the conception teachers have of their professional work. At the heart of it, students and advisors must design personal projects that revolutionize a community's view of what is possible. Personalized learning can grow into school transformation when all participants cross the boundaries that divide them to cocreate new expectations for secondary schools.

SCHOOL TRANSFORMATION THROUGH MUTUAL LEARNING

The fragmentation and isolation of human energy within a conventional high school make whole-school change a daunting enterprise. As Theodore Sizer said many times, "You have to change the whole system" to change any part. Not only do you have to unlock all the practices that tie the school into one system, but you also have to make all the changes concurrently, or lagging parts of the organization sap energy while active innovators burn themselves out. Engaging a whole community in high school personalization so change in one area supports adaptation in connected areas is, of course, impossible within a short time. When students, teachers, departments, student services, administrative offices, or political agencies remove themselves from the process of transformation, a personalization initiative loses the power to fulfill its aims. So, high school transformation has to be an ongoing effort, as all participants revise their assumptions and roles to fit patterns that emerge as policy, procedures, and practice rattle against each other only as they move toward coherence.

Several high schools across the country have established aspects of personalization separately, but tying many separate programs together systematically requires agreement among many people to focus energy on shared purposes rather than separate roles (DiMartino & Clarke, 2008).

The constraints against whole-school personalization are formidable:

- Students may balk at the prospect of taking responsibility for their learning.
- Teachers may argue that they are not trained as counselors.
- Trained in an academic discipline, teachers may not feel prepared for personalized courses.
- Some parents may get nervous if personalized studies crowd out conventional courses.

- Team teaching requires a kind of collaboration that limits individual prerogatives.
- Team design may shift power uncomfortably toward shared leadership within a school.
- Scheduling, budgeting, contracts, curriculum requirements, school rules, and a web of policies all favor putting groups into subject-based classes.

Against the tangle that forms the status quo, it is no wonder that whole-school personalization has taken place in charter schools, career academies, private schools, magnet schools, and other small settings designed at the beginning to be personalized institutions.

The term *alignment,* getting components of the system to connect to one purpose, has often been used to describe the work of secondary curriculum development and school improvement, but personalization cannot be achieved by lining things up mechanically, and it cannot be imposed by one part of a system on another. Change occurs when people show each other what they have made, provoking further adaptation. Transformation has to occur through mutual adaptation as members of the community build, recognize, and accept a shared vision of their work. Then they can bring different skills and knowledge to bear on the professional issues they face together. Collaboration under a shared vision generates new ideas. A shared vision grows as participants succeed and fail in efforts to realize their vision and develop their skills to take on new challenges.

GROWTH THROUGH INTERACTION

Too many school transformation initiatives have dropped down on schools and students from the top, only to dissipate when resistance gathers—while teachers invent a multitude of ways to let the current fad wash past them. Change from the top is depersonalized, so the people who need to change often remain disengaged, passive but compliant, or angry and dismissive. Mandated change leaves a persistently sour taste that usually increases when the next mandates appear, now in a setting that has already degraded its capacity to improve. Other transformation initiatives boil up from the bottom, as teachers and students discover new ways to learn and teach and come to believe their discoveries will improve learning. Bottom-up initiatives usually perish from starvation as the larger system simply carries out business as usual, leaving classroom-driven change out of the stream of consciousness and revenue.

Participants in large-scale change have to communicate across the lines that divide them into specialties, roles, and levels of hierarchy so they learn mutually about the constantly changing challenges they face. I decided to interview adults involved in school transformation at Mount Abraham, asking them to tell the story of their involvement in Pathways. As the graphic shows, I talked with people in different parts of the enterprise, from the state secretary of education to Pathways advisors, to see how their stories intertwined. In their stories, three observations stand out:

1. Each person had a similar view of the purpose of their work, a shared vision.

2. From separate vantage points, they brought unique talents to enacting their vision.

3. Interactions across barriers and boundaries supported adaptation of the vision and innovation among participants over the longer term.

Leadership occurs through interaction, and everybody must lead. The power to transform a school does not lie at the bottom or the top; it is shared among all of those who participate. "No" is still the most powerful word in education, and anybody can use it. Asking committed educators and other adults from across the community to look at ways to engage students in learning starts with a team that agrees to say "yes" to solutions they devise for themselves.

The excerpted interviews that follow show a pattern of connected work in showing how several participants in school transformation at Mount Abraham brought unique perspectives and talents into their interactions. Trying new ideas pressed them to continually modify their vision and fueled ongoing personalization at Mount Abraham (see Figure 7.1).

Figure 7.1   Perspectives on Pathways Transformation

Student Leaders
Logan Rotax, Grade 11

Evelyn Howard, ANESU District Superintendent
Policy and Systems Leaders
Nancy Cornell, ANESU Associate Superintendent, Curriculum

Andy Kepes, School Coprincipal and Middle School Exploratory Team
Transformation Leaders
Leon Wheeler, School Coprincipal

Perspectives on Transformation

Gerrie Heuts, Community Liaison
Pathways Advisors
Russell Comstock, Pathways Advisor

Caroline Camara, Pathways/Department Team Leader
Personalization Dept. Leaders
Maureen Deppman, Personalized Learning Team Leader

Armando Vileseca, Vermont Secretary of Education
State Policy Leaders

Via Interviews That Follow

REMOVING BARRIERS: ARMANDO VILASECA, VERMONT SECRETARY OF EDUCATION

Before he became secretary of education, Armando had worked as a high school principal and superintendent of schools aiming to engage all students in learning. As superintendent, he joined the leadership team of a statewide task force of more than 40 people from all walks of life, who produced the report *High Schools on the Move: Renewing Vermont's Commitment to Secondary Education,* adopted by the state board of education in 2002. The report coalesced various personalization experiments across the state. The Mount Abraham coprincipals cited the chapter "Twelve Principles for High School Renewal in Vermont" as a guiding document for school transformation at Mount Abraham (see Figure 7.2). After struggling to change high school learning for many years, Armando still spoke with animation about the complexity of redesigning high schools but also raised questions that still confound the process of transformation.

When I started as secretary, the State Board had begun to looking at transformation of education in Vermont, mostly focused on high schools. When I came in, I said that we already had a document that has what we want to accomplish. Let's use *High Schools on the Move* as a foundation, which had taken about 18 months to develop, with a broad range of folks involved. It is a model for high school redesign that is more reflective of meeting standards than doing seat time. Great idea! That's the easy part. If you ask most people working in schools about graduating by standards, they don't have a clue.

Title 16 of the Vermont Statutes related to education allows students to graduate either by meeting standards or completing Carnegie Units, with standards being the first option. It doesn't need my approval, but it has to be approved by local boards, according to local requirements. It can be done in multiple ways.

But, high schools operate in boxes. The bell rings. A thousand kids stand up move to the next 40- or 80-minute class, and when the bell rings again, they move to the next one. We can track and document their assumed progression in that manner. How do you make sure kids are engaged, seeing the relevance of what they are learning in a way that is also aligned with the requirements for college entrance? Colleges should want to see kids' real work.

How can you do this in an age where standards are becoming more concrete, when competence has to be achieved at a certain time, like in Algebra I? How can we help kids meet the standards for algebra and geometry in multiple ways, so a student can take algebra that is much more practical and applied, where kids are learning geometry and physics because they need to build something or take it apart?

How do we provide more sharing among schools? Can we get time in the contract for teachers to visit schools to see what's happening and get some mentoring? Can we come up with a three-semester model, with one semester being visioning and working with colleagues in learning groups and so we haven't lost any time with kids? How do we provide more sharing among schools? There have to be cohorts of kids we share, so we can decide to do things separately or together.

People agree on these concepts, but get hung up on the details, so they easily turn back to the older system that was clean and predictable—but not engaging. Traditional high schools need models, not just in a MET in Providence or an alternative program. People say, show me how to do it. I want to do it. I believe it. There are schools that are doing it. We need the stories. There needs to be time for teachers to figure this out.

Even after 10 years, the principals of Mount Abraham refer to *High Schools on the Move* as their guiding vision; Andy Kepes and Leon Wheeler, school coprincipals, could exploit that aging document in their explanation to the faculty.

High Schools on the Move: Renewing Vermont's Commitment to Quality Secondary Education was published in 2002, a

Figure 7.2   Twelve Principles for High School Renewal in Vermont

1 Engaged Learners
Students are engaged learners who are responsible for and actively involved in their own learning.

2 Challenging Standards
Each student is expected to demonstrate that he or she has met challenging standards based on *Vermont's Framework of Standards and Learning Opportunities* or national standards.

3 Multiple Pathways
High schools provide each student with a variety of learning opportunities and multiple pathways to meet graduation requirements.

4 Personalized Learning
High schools create small, personalized and safe learning environments that provide students with stable support from adults, caring connections to mentors, and a sense of belonging.

5 Flexible Structures
High school schedules and organizations are flexible to allow time for varied instructional activities and to provide an integrated learning experience. Learning is the constant; time is the variable.

6 Real-Life Experiences
Students learn about careers and college opportunities through real-life experiences and adult interaction, including work-based learning, service learning, career exploration, job shadowing, and career academies.

7 Instructional Leadership
Adults in the school use research-based practices and effective administrative and instructional strategies to support increased student performance.

8 Alignment
Supported by research-based professional development, high schools align their curricula, instruction, and assessment with Vermont's *School Quality Standards*.

9 Shared Purpose
Every high school adopts and publicizes a compelling vision and mission that uses a results-oriented approach to promote continuous improvement.

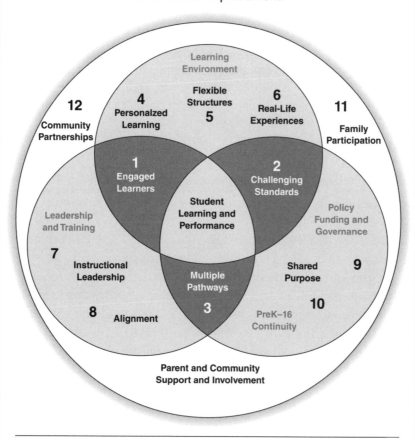

(Continued)

Figure 7.2 (Continued)

10 PreK–16 Continuity
Every high school is a member of a preK–16 education system and is a partner with middle schools, colleges, and postgraduation training programs to help students make successful transitions.

11 Family Participation
Families are active participants in their young adults' education and have varied opportunities to volunteer, serve on decision-making groups, assist students in setting learning goals, monitor results, and support learning at home.

12 Community Partnerships
Every high school forms active partnerships with families, community members, business people, civic leaders, and policymakers to ensure fiscal support and to expand student learning opportunities.

Source: Vermont Department of Education (2002). Used with permission.

little less than a decade ago. It's an amazing document! Almost everything our school is grappling with as we design our way forward to transformation is addressed, from personalized learning and multiple pathways to parent and community partnerships. . . . As I read *High Schools on the Move*, I'm awed by the vision it lays out and proud of the history of our school community, which is acknowledged in several categories as an "Example of Effective Practice." At the same time I'm deeply curious (on the verge of frustrated) about what happened that caused our educational progress toward this vision, both our school and the state, to stall for close to a decade. (Message from the principals, personal communication, 2011)

Four members of the Mount Abe community had served on the original Task Force.

SHAPING A SHARED VISION: EVELYN HOWARD, SUPERINTENDENT OF THE ADDISON NORTHEAST K–12 SCHOOL DISTRICT

By gathering a shared vision for the school district, K–12, Evelyn opened the door to participation from across the district. In a long series of community forums, she asked people from the Five Towns to meet in the cafeteria to establish a foundation of shared values, which she converted to a list of outcome targets for all the schools, "ends policies" guiding change across the district, K–12. Through a process of "policy governance," she then prepared six school boards to focus their work on policy development and progress monitoring, while leaving program development and management to the professional staff. Teachers and administrators were empowered to innovate, while the school board and community looked for evidence of progress toward 12 stated "ends" in three major groupings (see Figure 7.3). Pathways reflects all of these goals. Early, she sponsored the development of a video about Pathways to be shown around the community, at conferences, and at school board meetings. She also arranged times for Pathways students and teachers to bring students to school board meetings to show their work, so they could see the three "ends" coming to life.

The Ends Statements [Figure 7.3] came out of focus forums held in each of the six school districts in this supervisory union. For four or five years, we gathered people together to think about what the 21st century may offer and what is different and the same about now and the past. The focus forums were specially designed to get a forward-looking perspective on what it is we want kids to know and be able to do, about what kinds of experience would contribute to that, and how the community could support that kind of learning for students.

In all the schools, there was an overwhelming desire for kids to discover their strengths, be recognized for their strengths, be nurtured toward using those personal attributes to be productive, and contribute to society. When we talk about what is most important, the community wants the students to blossom. They all want students to feel good about who they are, what they can do, what their potential might be and be hopeful about their future. They want the public schools to personalize learning for students.

When we started the Pathways program, we took every opportunity we had to show individual stories of success through nontraditional means and brought those stories

Figure 7.3   Three Main Groupings for Twelve District "Ends"

1. *Core Subjects in a Digital and Global Environment:* To become one's personal best and a contributing member of a community, each student will demonstrate knowledge and skills within and across disciplines.

2. *Life and Career Skills:* To become one's personal best and a contributing member of a community, each student will develop effective social and emotional skills.

3. *Learning and Innovation Skills:* To become one's personal best and a contributing member of a community, each student will develop skills that lead to using one's mind well.

Source: Addison Northeast Supervisory Union and member school districts (Bristol, Lincoln, Monkton, Mt. Abraham Union High, New Haven, Starksboro).

back to the school board and the community. The stories let everyone see new possibilities. Pathways students can celebrate their discovery in the same way that other students find interesting and challenging work in the traditional classroom where skillful teachers personalize learning for all students.

One of the things that I have observed in moving ahead is that the principals and the Transformation Team need to think ahead more about how things could be different before they start to put routine things in place. I think we have to do more thinking in advance about how to grow personalized learning before routine scheduling governs and restricts ways for more staff to innovate, contribute, participate, and share in the success of the change. I am also looking for ways that others can contribute directly and become part of the Pathways program. When you surround yourself with really committed people, you are not building a picture in isolation; you are building the possibilities collectively.

At the high school, I am asking for people to step up and step out, to think about how they might contribute, even in a small way, to the idea that each student comes with personal potential, and the more we can help them know that potential, the better and stronger they will be when they leave us as high school graduates.

LINKING PERSONALIZATION TO EXISTING MODELS: NANCY CORNELL, ASSOCIATE SUPERINTENDENT FOR CURRICULUM, INSTRUCTION, AND ASSESSMENT

In a standards-based system that is also personalized, it may be necessary to reorder curriculum priorities. Recently, competencies have been written as required subjects that organize specific skills and knowledge specific enough to be tested reliably. Often, standards documents can fill an entire booklet. "Less is more," as Theodore and Nancy Sizer insisted when they started the Coalition of Essential Schools. In the Mount Abraham District, the five competency areas organize the required outcomes for graduation, while other documents describe enabling standards connected to subject-area knowledge that teachers can use to arrange their courses and assessment process (see Figure 7.4). Teachers are encouraged to use content areas to enable students to meet the Five Competencies and Ends Statements, which are the graduation requirements. Associate Superintendent Nancy Cornell has been finding ways to connect personalized assessment with earlier models.

> We are working on figuring out together what a personalized and standards-based curriculum and assessment system looks like, with our school district's rather global 21st century–like "Ends Policy" as a foundation. We are learning how to engage kids across the school and how to build curriculum around their interests and concerns, while also giving them concrete models of projects and performances that meet standards. The district "Ends Goals" encourage all teachers to focus on a few outcomes K–12, and those outcomes take precedence over externally imposed goals. [See Figure 7.3.]
>
> If you start with the End Goal that kids need to be able to research something and write persuasively about it, the topic doesn't have to be about the War of 1812. On the other hand, you can't research and write persuasively about nothing. You need topics and need to understand them thoroughly to write well about them. The question is, who chooses the topics?
>
> Technology has a huge part to play in this, putting a bunch of disengaged students in a room with unfettered access to computers. That has made so much possible that was not possible before. There are teachers in the school who created a website where they put readings for each other. I think that we will always have courses, but there is a challenge in helping people envision ways to personalize learning in a regular course. [See Figure 7.5.]

Figure 7.4 ANESU Curriculum Structure

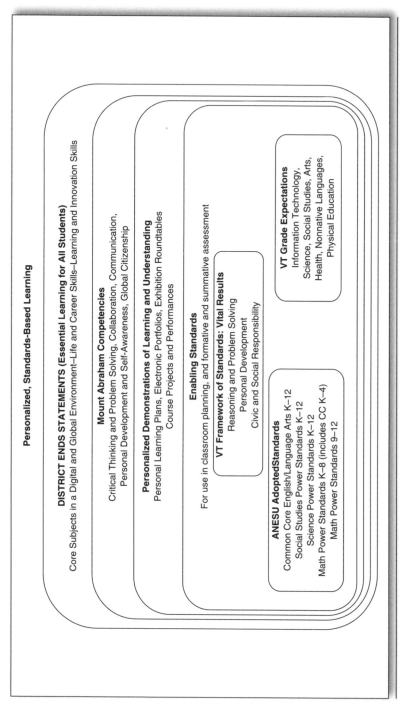

Personalized, Standards-Based Learning

DISTRICT ENDS STATEMENTS (Essential Learning for All Students)
Core Subjects in a Digital and Global Environment–Life and Career Skills–Learning and Innovation Skills

Mount Abraham Competencies
Critical Thinking and Problem Solving, Collaboration, Communication,
Personal Development and Self-Awareness, Global Citizenship

Personalized Demonstrations of Learning and Understanding
Personal Learning Plans, Electronic Portfolios, Exhibition Roundtables
Course Projects and Performances

Enabling Standards
For use in classroom planning, and formative and summative assessment

VT Framework of Standards: Vital Results
Reasoning and Problem Solving
Personal Development
Civic and Social Responsibility

ANESU AdoptedStandards
Common Core English/Language Arts K–12
Social Studies Power Standards K–12
Science Power Standards K–12
Math Power Standards K–8 (includes CC K–4)
Math Power Standards 9–12

VT Grade Expectations
Information Technology,
Science, Social Studies, Arts,
Health, Nonnative Languages,
Physical Education

179

It's a scary prospect for lots of us who were not educated this way and who have spent many years teaching a curriculum that we can define in advance, while being settled enough with ambiguity and uncertainty that we keep going and figure it out together. As we are hiring, we want to be thoughtful about seeking out people who have experience with personalized learning or who have a fire in their bellies and are willing to come on the adventure.

To engage classroom teachers in the schoolwide initiative, she developed a process for personalizing conventional courses (see Figure 7.5).

Figure 7.5   Process for Personalizing Courses

1. Choose a *competency area* to focus on.

2. Choose a kind of *task* in that area.

3. Develop a generic (not task-specific) *schoolwide rubric* (using standards as a resource to describe the rubric dimensions and points on the rubric).

4. Identify the kinds of *student work* we deem most important (could be done by all departments and grades, or selected departments and grades).

5. Collect/develop models of the tasks. *Annotate those models* using the schoolwide rubric (standards-based).

6. Design and implement *targeted practice* using those models and the schoolwide rubric.

7. Design and implement *emotional triggers* that engage students in this type of task.

8. Give students *rapid feedback* on their targeted practice, using the schoolwide rubric or elements of the schoolwide rubric.

9. *Collect evidence* (How are kids doing?), and use this evidence to refine targeted practice, emotional trigger, and feedback.

10. Collect and *share annotated models,* and classroom examples of targeted practice and emotional triggers that worked.

11. *Refine* schoolwide rubric.

12. *Refine models;* align models "horizontally" (across subjects within a grade) and "vertically" (is the level of challenge increasing appropriately through the grades?).

13. *Design a system* for knowing where (in what courses), the models and targeted practice are being used.

14. Design a system for *reporting student progress* in this type of task.

Source: Copyright © ANESU. Used with permission.

Courses will still make up the largest part of a personalized curriculum, but they too can be designed to prepare students to meet schoolwide standards.

CONTINUOUS ADAPTATION THROUGH ENGAGED LEADERSHIP

Working with the Transformers team, Mount Abraham's coprincipals, Andy Kepes and Leon Wheeler, wrote three simple guidelines emphasizing personalization rather than test scores as the basis for transformation (see Figure 7.6).

Andy's approach to transformation is to keep the vision at the forefront while engaging himself with people who are actively changing the system.

Andy Kepes, school coprincipal and teacher in the Middle School Exploratory team, made interaction with both faculty and students a daily exercise.

Figure 7.6   Vision for Mount Abraham Transformation Initiative

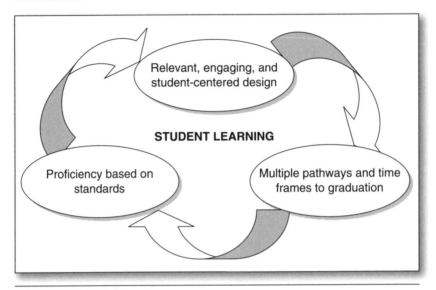

Source: Reprinted with permission from Mount Abraham Union Middle High School, Bristol, Vermont.

When you have two coexisting systems, traditional education and Pathways in the same space, they pull at each other. If you go to a school like the MET, you find that personalization is all they are doing. Somebody said, you have to make change fast enough so gravity does not pull you back down. You want Pathways to pull the traditional system along, but sometimes I think tradition is pulling Pathways, drawing in diversions. A separate little school is different. We are unique because we are working inside a large school.

Traditional teachers are skeptical sometimes and wonder what is going on—and maybe not agreeing with what is going on. Compliance and engagement are two different things. At Mount Abraham, you can personalize from 17 percent (one class out of six) to 100 percent—one class per day to four classes a day. That has started turning people around.

Carnegie Units and letter grades have to go by the wayside. Philosophically I can take any teacher and they will agree that grades and Carnegie Units are stupid. But when the rubber meets the road, they struggle: "I have always given my students one hundred questions about content, and that's how I arrive at a grade Now you are asking me to give a grade on how they collaborate, and how they problem-solve or communicate." I talk about depth to another science teacher. I say, just don't cover all the topics. She says she has to cover all the subjects. Why, how long will students remember those factoids?

While Andy serves as a coprincipal, keeping the conversation alive across the school, he also teaches a middle school exploratory course introducing a Pathways approach to independent learning.

We have the two skateboard boys. I was battling just to keep them on topic—on anything. And then I got lucky. They were working on a logo, and they wanted me just to buy a skateboard they had designed online, for $40 or $80. I said, no you can't do that. You just used a CAD design program to design a board online. What if you had an old skateboard deck? Bring it in and sand it down to wood. You guys are going to design the board and then put a logo on it. "We can do that?" "Yes, you can." Suddenly, they are stopping me in the hall, asking, "Can we do this or do that on the skateboard?"

Andy can explain it because he is doing it. In school transformation, working on organization and working with students inform each other—and learning becomes mutual.

ORGANIZING TEAMS AND STRUCTURES: LEON WHEELER, MOUNT ABRAHAM COPRINCIPAL

Leon Wheeler began his work at Mount Abraham persuaded that test-oriented teaching would govern high school learning forever. Paradoxically, the high school's turn toward personalization was an indirect effect of its being labeled as "failing" under No Child Left Behind.

> The requirement to have states hold local schools to a common standard and show continual improvement in student progress was noble, but flawed. Soul searching has ultimately led us to the very things we lost during this past decade: personalized, individualized learning that compels each student to find their interests and build their dreams. Now, we're working to make our transformation schoolwide.
>
> The statewide test scores (NECAP) are a measure of something, but if you focus on improving the NECAP scores, you still may not get to the point where students have any connection to the learning itself. Not just knowledge and good grades; they have to feel that the preparation they have had in school has made them ready to do something that matters. I had to wrap my head around this. Not alone, but with a group of others.
>
> Any transformation has to happen in a community—within a team structure, initially just a planning team for Pathways. Then we added a team called the Umbrella team. They thought less about the content of learning but more about the supports and structures that engage kids more deeply in the learning process. Pathways paved the way, modeling a path of rethinking what education can look like.
>
> The Personalized Learning Department has expanded as we have worked on engaging kids deeply in designing their own pathways to graduation and on personalizing learning in ways that matter to them. As teachers think about embedding 21st century skills in their content areas, what Pathways is learning can be transferred to their classrooms, creating new opportunities, a transformation—a paradigm shift. [See Figure 7.6.]
>
> We don't want to ask people to do things they don't have the skills to do. At the same time, we don't want to

> stifle creativity. We want teachers to take risks. Through smaller team learning, we increase learning in the whole school about engaging kids. I think teachers are craving the challenge. If the administration has to control the change, it won't happen. How do we measure enthusiasm? How can we tap in to that? We need continuous feedback on what is working. That will force us to keep changing until we get it right.

As the Transformation Group began converting Pathways processes for schoolwide application, they designed a general scheme for standards-based curriculum and instruction, whether in single classes, interdisciplinary teams, or "gateway" tasks that move students from one grade to another.

Unifying Personalized Learning: Caroline Camara and Maureen Deppman, Cochairs of Personalized Learning Department

As personalized learning gained momentum in the school, integration offered a way for the school to open a wide spectrum of options for all students, whether they wanted to design a fully personalized curriculum or a half credit in an area of interest. The Personalized Learning Department merged Pathways Program to create an wide array of personalized opportunities:

Weaving Choices Into Coherent Patterns: Maureen Deppman

> *The Middle School Exploratory courses* have been around for seven years. I taught two courses, one of which has now become a *mini-Pathways course,* while Bill Connor teaches eight sections of a *Personal Learning Plan Exploratory (PLP)* based on five questions:
>
> Who am I?
>
> What is my history?

What are my dreams?

What are my fears?

What are my goals?

Andy [the principal], Caroline, and I now teach the Middle School Pathways Exploratory, with about 19 students each quarter. We introduce the *Independent Learning Skills* and start with a less risky project, on cooking, where they learn the skills, and then they pick their own projects, 19 students and 19 projects. Some of our mentors are Pathways students, such as Asher, who is working with some younger students on video technology.

The PLP and portfolio go hand in hand. The PLP is a rough draft, and the portfolio is your best work that you show to colleges or employers. We are working with Guidance to convert the form they use to write recommendations and then move it to the portfolio site and change the PLP to do that job.

We have a seen a big boom in *Virtual High School.* To start, we received 15 blocks of virtual course work, but we got more applications so we increased to 20, then added two more, and now we have more students asking for next year. We discovered this year that all eighth graders taking virtual courses have asked to enroll again in the ninth grade. They are also taking courses such as animal behavior, mythology, AP courses like calculus, AP European History, Russian and Italian, bioethics, biotechnology, and Irish contemporary literature. We have a pretty rigorous application process for virtual courses, including a survey on independent learning, and because of that our students are very successful in the courses.

We worked over one summer to create *Independent Learning Opportunities* (ILOs) where students can now earn core credits in English, science, social studies, rather than pass/fail credit through independent studies. When Caroline and I designed the ILOs, we got 23 kids for a six-kid pilot. The ILO contract is aligned with the core competencies, including a student-led conference and exhibition, working more closely with an advisor or mentor.

Dual enrollment in college courses is expanding. The Community College of Vermont (CCV) offers a free Introduction to College course, and kids who complete that get a free voucher for another CCV course, sometimes over the summer. A student who graduated last year had enough credits to enroll at Syracuse University as a sophomore. A couple of our students take college technology courses. One of our students, a ninth grader, has taken two community colleges courses. We have a student taking three courses at the University of Vermont, hoping to enroll in the School of Engineering.

EXPANDING ROLES FOR TEACHERS:
CAROLINE CAMARA, DEPARTMENT COCHAIR

Engaging the faculty remains a challenge for school transformation as well as for independent student projects. The school has not chosen to prescribe personalized roles for individual teachers, but instead lets teacher engagement evolve as appropriate. As befits any personalized setting, teacher involvement takes forms that fit an immediate need. Some mentoring teachers simply consult with a student once or twice about a single question, serving in a consulting role. Others might suggest readings or check in with a student during a semester. A mentoring teacher might meet regularly with one or two students and participate in exhibitions. Some set up internships for students or adapt courses to a project-based format. When teachers do not conceive of their engagement as a defined set of responsibilities, they might hesitate to work with a student at all, and their preconceptions would probably limit what they think should be done.

Caroline spoke about the variety of roles teachers were taking under their own sense of personalization as a vision:

Greg Clark [social studies] is doing senior Age of Legality as an ILO, but with a flexible schedule. The students do the same assignments as others, and he meets with five seniors once a week. With our kids, he had a big conversation about the process. What did you go through to get this done? So now, Greg is saying, I am going to take this process back to my classroom from now on. The next day, he started the new process in a regular class.

Sam Kayhart is working with an ILO about a project where the student acts as an assistant teacher in biology. Sam is so excited, helping the kid establish a project, establish what she wanted to learn, feeding in some content and skills. She has picked up a bit more content than in a typical ILO. Another teacher has taken up physical therapy with a student who is interested. Her questions are mostly about career options but they include, "How do muscles and the skeleton work?"

We have a student doing an ILO outside of school, a ninth grader. [He is] learning how to program servomotors, [and] learning how to create an autonomous vehicle with his uncle. He said to me last week, "I just finished building the car. Now it's time to work on the programming." I can't be his content mentor in this case. I am asking the uncle to come in and become the content mentor. I do the credits, but he is the expert in the field.

Just as students grow projects to explore their interests, teachers grow an approach to personalization that fits their lives.

ADVISING WHILE REDESIGNING PATHWAYS: RUSSELL COMSTOCK, ACADEMIC ADVISOR

Russell Comstock joined the Pathways design team as a member of the community who had experience in outdoor education, emergency medicine, and ecology and then became an advisor. He has worked with the Pathways team adapting and refining the program over three years.

> My days balance between working directly with the students, some of whom are spending more time in the Pathways room, some who are out. I check in with them, reviewing where they are on their projects, trying to spur their thinking. And the other side of the work is administrative, looking at work they have handed in or corresponding with parents—sending e-mails or exploring a topic so I can come back to the students with a response. Rapid feedback is very important to them.
>
> I find the most meaningful time is when I am interacting with students.
>
> "What really captivates you?" I ask. "Put together some kind of construct about how you see the world. You may be oriented toward farming or mechanics, where your attention is focused." The strength of this program is that students can design academic inquiry, which becomes the inquiry of self. "Who am I? What can I contribute to the community?"
>
> Our initial purpose at Pathways was to find a way to engage students who were disengaged, who might have been getting ready to drop out, and who were a drain of energy on the educational system. During our first eight months of planning, we visited other schools, read some books, and drafted a framework—with lots and lots of conversation. We can now show how we engage students who would otherwise drop out or who are just not interested in traditional learning.
>
> Even though we felt we began with a pretty solid concept, it was fascinating to see what changed when it was time to apply that concept. There were a whole lot of things we hadn't sorted out yet, but we went ahead and got a pilot going. There were four of us, and we worked in an egalitarian way. There was a lot of "Let's try this thing. Yes! Let's do it! Yeah. Let's do it! Try this! Try that!"

We found we were always incomplete in the things we were trying to track. An example would be figuring out how to spark, sustain, and document the work of each student. We were flying by the seat of our pants. Our number-one goal was to keep them engaged, give them opportunities to see that the world is fascinating. We would figure out awarding credits after the fact—how to get written work, and what is needed to graduate. We had ideas, but they were not fully thought out or in place. We went through that semester, exhausted ourselves, had a great time—and we had full engagement.

We had to make an effort to get all students out of our classroom, connected to the community. There were just a few students who had not figured out yet how to do that, or experienced the joy of active learning, where you get involved with something that really interests you. What kept them in this space was not yet having internalized an understanding of how to advocate for themselves or take initiative. It's not that they were resistant; it was just that they didn't know what was possible yet—that by dreaming up something and going to find Gerrie they could be out in the community with someone two or three times a week.

We discovered that we needed many, many more stepping-stones, clear and concrete. We developed a rubric for "independent learning," designed to help them see their own growth. We asked them to read three books per quarter. They had to choose books from three categories, something of their own choice, something from their project areas, and something from a list of classics. Then, once they read, they had a long list of ways they could create a reading response. Or, they could propose a way of their own. We wrote up models of different kinds of responses, whether it was rewriting the end of the story, or doing a diorama, changing the setting of the story, or building a model from what they read. We had them do an end-of-the-semester reflection from four prompts, combining all they had read. We showed them a graphic organizer, with questions in a flow—and a model of what they could do. We were gradually redesigning Pathways in a new format.

MUTUAL RENEWAL

What teacher has not watched a student begin the year in lethargy but gain momentum as old ideas connect with new ideas, generating movement in a new direction? The same phenomenon occurs among teachers. Every school has its pioneers, people who are actively searching for ideas that promise to engage students. Scheduling some pioneers into a planning period with others who might be interested period can give birth to a team, such as the middle-level and ninth-grade teams at Mount Abraham. A little soft funding for road trips, materials, conferences, summer workshops, or paid team time brings different talents into one space. The best way to create a team is to put people in a car and send them somewhere.

Personalization cannot be relegated to a committee. A committee is a group empowered to make decisions on behalf of others. A team, conversely, is a group of people joined together to change their own practices, making changes happen in daily work. Committees usually focus on policies and procedures; teams tend to focus on practice, particularly if they include teachers and students. Teams are a better medium for ongoing school transformation, because team members may have little power over others but can be given extensive control over their own daily work. Transformation depends on teams working out solutions to the problems they face separately in enacting a shared vision. Even leadership becomes a team effort. Only though interaction can they learn enough to make a difference.

In a change process that depends on continuous interactions among people with distinctive talents and a shared purpose, withdrawing from creative interactions can prove lethal. The loudest way to say no is to say nothing at all, going limp, or smiling and dropping into "compliance mode." Personalizing a high school involves growing a new culture from a pre-existing culture that holds established practices in place. The process occurs when innovations in in one realm trigger reconsideration and change in neighboring realms in ways that help people in both realms better understand the nature of the culture they are growing collaboratively. Participants in school transformation have to accept change as part of their work and understand the nature of the process in which they are engaged:

- No single individual can guide the process of growth from a single vantage point; participants guide themselves as their awareness grows.
- Changing a school culture ignites fear and passion, which need to be channeled into experimentation and collaboration.
- Early changes and ideas may prove surprisingly obsolescent as personalization spreads throughout a school community.
- Although ideas and techniques can be imported from elsewhere, transformation rests on local initiatives that involve students, teachers, school administrators, and policy developers.
- All participants have to act as leaders who carry news of success and failure from one realm to the next and help connect their innovations to the larger transformation.
- Disorganization and confusion are inevitable in any changing system, signaling the need for even more communication and collaboration.

Clearly, school transformation involves weaving a coherent pattern of relationships from a tangle of different threads. The pattern emerges slowly through personal interactions.

Nagging Questions About High School Transformation

1. State and national policies lean heavily against personalized or customized learning. How much campaigning will it take to open the policy environment to personalized learning?

2. Testing companies, text publishers, local employers, and school boards have a vested interest in keeping things as they are. Who can take responsibility for political change to make room for personalized learning?

3. Many high schools have a hierarchical structure; most personalized processes depend on leadership distributed across boundaries. How can we begin to reconfigure school leadership so students and teachers can make the adaptations they need to make?

4. Teachers choose their profession based on affiliations to a particular subject area. Their training includes class planning, curriculum design, testing, and classroom management. Many see advising as counseling and feel unprepared to manage individual relationships. Not all are confirmed risk takers. How can we help teachers prepare for new roles in personalized learning?

5. Many students have learned that passivity and anonymity ensure safety. What will it take to persuade more students to take control of their own learning in a more public arena?

6. Current management systems—schedules, buses, grading, faculty assignments, hiring, budgeting, and record keeping—are based on the assumption that all students will proceed through similar experiences in a coordinated fashion. What will it take to adjust those systems so they support wider variability?

7. How can we define accountability in a personalized high school?

8. The cofounders of the Met, as well as innovators such as Ted and Nancy Sizer, believed that students need to learn in a "smaller learning community" with only 100 to 200 students. Pathways is designed to engage the whole school. What problems will large size cause for schoolwide transformation?

Conclusion

From Knowledge to Power

When I began teaching, tracking was basic to the way high schools organized curriculum and instruction. Advanced Placement students received excellent instruction in advanced subjects; honors students received a classical education from accomplished scholars; general students received an assortment of experiences from competent instructors; and noncollege-bound students received whatever a creative teacher might assemble to capture their attention. My honors classes were effortless; my classes with noncollege-bound students were a challenge. I tried to lead them into reading and writing by bringing up "big questions" and heating them up on one side or the other so they would put energy into academic skills development. I do not remember asking any of my students how they wanted to conduct their lives.

High schools serve multiple purposes in our society. Two of them stand out because they so often confound each other:

- *Personal empowerment:* High schools prepare young students to use information to manage their minds and lives.
- *Sorting and selecting:* High schools provide the society with young people to fill the roles it relies on for continuation.

In retrospect, I wonder why we put so much effort into sorting and selecting when young adults themselves are perfectly capable of using their education to make their own way, with our support.

SORT AND SELECT OR EMPOWER TO GROW?

I see myself in many of the students I have met in Pathways. I find myself asking how I would be different if I had used my schooling to meet the Mount Abraham Competencies rather than to go for high grades, good scores, and the safety of staying on the beaten path. I deeply admire the young adults who take their search seriously for a kind of knowledge they see as essential to their freedom, a purpose I never fulfilled in school. I see in these young people a kind of courage I never had to take on risks and to understand their world while struggling with uncertainty. That challenge promises pain but offers self-respect in return.

Although students in conventional classes would probably describe their experience of a semester in a similar way, students in a personalized program have to look at the world they have designed for themselves. Their purpose is their own, evolving along the path of their discovery. Their semester plans resemble no others. They read different books, experience different parts of their community, talk to different people, and collect different kinds of evidence that shows how they have met program standards. Only in meeting common standards does their experience reflect commonality—a demonstrated ability to meet adult challenges. Forging their own pathways, they begin to use their creativity, curiosity, and aspirations to improve their lives and the lives of others.

Personalized learning organizes a different voyage for each student. Each becomes a navigator, and a high school helps arrange a ship and a crew. Not every voyage takes the same amount of time. Not all voyages are happy. Kieran enrolled in Pathways for a year before taking a course at the National Outdoor Leadership Experience and then choosing to finish high school at the Walden Project, an alternative pathway toward graduation offered by a neighboring school district. Walden students take classes, explore their community, and conduct projects based in a rough tent in the woods far beyond a cornfield. Kieran's time at Pathways was not without angst, but it was critically important to the hopes he had begun to fashion for himself.

Looking for a quiet place to talk, Kieran and I found a plug for my recorder in an empty stairwell behind the auditorium, an echo chamber undisturbed by voices in the roiling hallways. Unlike other students whom I interviewed at Pathways, Kieran had prepared in advance for our conversation by compiling a list of six factors that would improve learning in a high school such as ours—the same task I had also begun in beginning this book. He handed me his list of descriptors for a school that would respond to the needs of young adults:

Kieran (11th Grade)

This a chart of student needs. It was designed to help me think. If change is going to come and progress happens, every kid is going to get involved.

Independence

Influence over the environment (which is what we absorb)

Respect

Equality

Comfort

Progress

Learning

Independence will have to come from the kids.

I have always had a pretty big problem with school and being schooled. It has been difficult for me to just sit down in rows of desks and watch the front of the class with a glazed stare, not really absorbing anything except for what

I have to do to just get by. I was going to drop out of high school this year. I am a very stubborn person. I said to myself, "This stuff is not worthwhile, I am not going to retain it. What is the point of learning it—just wasting my time, and my money, my effort—my life at that point? Why should I go on?"

But, getting a GED [general equivalency diploma] is not the same at all as getting your diploma, which is a real shame. I am not a good high school student at all. There are a lot of people who are the same as me, who grew up in the woods and mountains and learned everything by doing it—rather than just looking at it. My infatuation with learning started when a friend of mine said to me, "I really think you have the ability to mind-**** this system— or change it." I said, "Why not?" I got into Pathways. And I started to find things that made me adamant about learning. It's so simple. I should have gotten it, but I didn't. I am growing up, and I am growing to be my own person.

Teachers have become just the regulators in the flow of knowledge. If you interact with a kid like he's lower than you, he will think that is all right, and he'll go and do the same thing to others. It will be a terrible cycle. Kids need to sit down and have an equal conversation with a teacher, speak to him like any other person. Influence grows like little drops of water. I would love to sit down and talk with a teacher like I have with one of my close friends. Everyone coexists and has to be interlocked to work. But you still need independence.

Personally, I just started trying this year. I had never tried in public school, never had to, and never [had] a reason to. Then I came to Pathways to do all these things and still learn. That was confusing as hell. That took so much thought, with the guidance of the Pathways people and the people I had known—and kids who graduated. I respect each one of the advisors wholeheartedly and the things they have done to make this program successful. Russell has done great things in getting me to a better place, by being calm and making a comfortable environment, something we lack in public school. Right now, I have zero credits at the high school. I sort of did this on purpose. I have always thought if you put yourself in hard situations, if you come out high or low, you still end up learning. I don't think I am going to drop out.

Where I live, everyone is part of the community. Especially in the mountain towns, the places where people learn the most about themselves and the woods. Where people respect them for being a person and people will help each other. You heard about the floods in the Northeast Kingdom. I drove by and people were trying to move a house. If your neighbor needs help, you help them. There was mud up to my knees, then my thighs. They had 27 people come out to completely clean up their farm. They had seven different farms donate plants. They are going to till it all up and plant again.

At Pathways, we got this community. Just as the Pathways community grew, all of these kids went out into the Bristol community. I entered the Bristol bakery and learned how to become a baker. I learned how to be a bee-keeper. I am going to help Russ Conrad build a cordwood house—on a work exchange. I am getting all this from the community, from building off of what I have learned and using the resources I have through other people, talking, and sharing and talking about what I want to do.

I trained to be a beekeeper. I had taken 20 pages of notes. Bees are so cool. Did you know honey is an antibac-terial; you can put raw honey on a cut. I learned how to be a hip-hop DJ, scratching and mixing records. I learned how to set a rhythm. I could see my progression, from not being able to do anything at all. I could mix polar opposite songs with a nice beat. Everything came together. It's a skill I learned. Who wants to do serious work all the time? When you are making music, you have the ability to be completely independent and creative. I started my year off just writing poetry, playing my guitar, and sitting by the river. Through that, I learned it's not worth doing nothing.

We started out at Pathways with a lot of freedom. It's been a year of almost complete personal growth for me. Since this is a personalized program, I have spent a lot of time with my thoughts. I have had to be responsible for myself and my own work, designing my own curriculum and getting credits for it, to use these resources and community. Pathways made it so I didn't drop out. It made me learn what I wanted to do with my life, and I have now some conviction, some determination to get into it. I have surpassed success. I am just way past success. That inspiration did come from being an independent person in the Pathways program. A passing grade in this school is a D. That's like just one letter grade away from an F. You can pass without doing any work. I wrote a page and a half last week on a writing prompt. I haven't done that in years.

For my exhibition, I prepared breads and two pastries, and croissants. I started at 9:50 to make a loaf of rye and French white. I did cinnamon buns and a royal icing with condensed milk that is sugared, a great icing. The croissants, we mixed in egg yolk, and [I] painted them with egg white. I guess what I did is to add too much jam, but they poofed out and jam was all over. I woke up at 5:00 and cooked it all. I came down and presented the entire thing from memory.

I am probably going to work with the Youth Conservation Corps next year. My brother has been working on trails. I have done trail work myself. I am trying to build a résumé for myself right now so once I get out of high school, it will say I am a hard worker. You're going to want me on your trail crew. I got wilderness first aid. I got certified at 16. I am going to for my first responder certification soon. I want to build these skills and keep adding to them. This is all just personal learning. Pathways say everybody has a worth and that everybody can say whatever they need to. Hopefully, I will be able to help others—my own kids and others.

I do think I have progressed. I made a lot of personal decisions. My dad told me that you shouldn't reinvent the wheel. I strongly feel I will have to reinvent the wheel. I want to look my kid in the eye and say, "Reinvent the wheel if you need to. From that, you will learn. I don't know what will happen to you. I am terrified, but I know that you will learn. The best teacher is yourself." Through this whole experience, I realized that with all this freedom, I could not make myself learn. I couldn't have anyone else make me learn. I had to fall in love with knowledge and change my entire view of what a school system is so I might improve someone else's experience and better my own.

Bibliography

Center for Collaborative Education. (2006). *Results from the Boston pilot schools study*. Boston: Center for Collaborative Education.

Clarke, J. (1999, April). Planting the seeds of systemic change. *NASSP Bulletin, 83*, 1–9.

Clarke, J. (2003a). *Personalized learning: An introduction*. Providence, RI: The Education Alliance at Brown University. Retrieved from http://www.alliance.brown.edu/pubs/changing_systems/introduction/index.php.

Clarke, J. (2003b). *Personalized learning: Personal learning plans, portfolios and presentations*. Providence, RI: The Education Alliance at Brown University. Retrieved from http://www.alliance.brown.edu/pubs/changing_systems/personalized_learning/.

Clarke, J. (2003). Personalized learning and personalized teaching. In J. DiMartino, J. Clarke, & D. Wolk (Eds.), *Personalized learning: preparing high school students to create their futures* (pp. 69–86). Lanham, MD: Scarecrow Press.

Clarke, J., Aiken, J. A., & Sullivan, M. J. (1999). Interactive leadership in high school reform. *NASSP Bulletin, 83*, 607.

Clarke, J., & Frazer, E. (2003). Making learning personal: Educational practices that work. In J. DiMartino, J. Clarke, & D. Wolk (Eds.), *Personalized learning: Preparing high school students to create their futures* (pp. 174–193). Lanham, MD: Scarecrow Press.

Cuban, L. (2012). Standards versus customization: Finding the balance. *Educational Leadership, 69*(5), 10–15.

Cushman, K. (1997). Why small schools are essential. *Coalition of Essential Schools, 13*(3). Retrieved from http://www.essentialschools.org/resources/21.

Darling-Hammond, L. (2002, January 18). *Redesigning schools for the 21st century*. Presentation given to the faculty of Hillsdale High School, Stanford University, San Mateo, CA.

Darling-Hammond, L., Ancess, J., & Ort, S. W. (2002). Outcomes of the coalition campus schools project. *American Educational Research Journal, 39*(3), 639–673.

DiMartino, J. (2003). Definition of personalized learning. In J. Clarke (Ed.), *Changing systems to personalize learning* (pp. 7–8). Providence, RI: The Education Alliance at Brown University.

DiMartino, J., & Clarke, J. (2008). *Personalizing the high school experience for each student.* Alexandria, VA: ASCD.

DiMartino, J., & Wolk, D. (2010). *The personalized high school: Making learning count for adolescents.* San Francisco: Jossey-Bass.

Geiser, S., & Santelices, M. V. (2007). *Validity of high-school grades in predicting student success beyond the freshman year: High-school record vs. standardized tests as indicators of four-year college outcomes* (Research & Occasional Paper Series: CSHE.6.07). Berkeley: Center for Studies in Higher Education, University of California, Berkeley. Retrieved from http://cshe.berkeley.edu/publica tions/docs/ROPS.GEISER._SAT_6.13.07.pdf.

Lee, V., & Smith, J. (1994). High school restructuring and student achievement: A new study finds strong links. *Issues in Restructuring Schools, 7*(1–5), 16. Madison, WI: Center on Organization and Restructuring of Schools.

Lee, V., Smith. J., & Croninger, R. (1995). Another look at high school restructuring. *Issues in Restructuring Schools* (Report #9). Madison, WI: Center on Organization and Restructuring of Schools.

Levine, E. (1993). *One kid at a time: Big lessons from a small school.* New York: Teachers College Press.

Littky, D. (2004). *The big picture: Education is everyone's business.* Alexandria, VA: ASCD.

Littky, D., & Allen, F. (1999). Whole school personalization: One student at a time. *Educational Leadership, 57*(1), 24–29.

McCombs, B., & Whisler, J. (1997). *The learner-centered classroom and school: Strategies for increasing student motivation and achievement.* San Francisco: Jossey-Bass.

Metropolitan Career and Technical Center. (2003). *Student learning in schools: An online portfolio.* Providence RI: Author.

National Commission on Excellence in Education, (1983). *A nation at risk: A report to the nation.* Washington, DC: U.S. Government Printing Office.

Newmann, F., Wehlage, G., & Lamborn, S. (1992). The significance and sources of student engagement. In F. M. Newmann (Ed.),

Student engagement and achievement in American secondary schools (pp. 11–30). New York: Teachers College Press.

North Central Regional Educational Laboratory. (2003). *enGauge: 21st century skills for 21st century learners.* Naperville, IL: Author. Retrieved from http://www.unctv.org/education/teachers_childcare/nco/documents/skillsbrochure.pdf.

Partnership for 21st Century Skills. (n.d.). *Framework for 21st century learning.* Retrieved from http://www.p21.org/overview/skills-framework.

Personalized Learning Foundation. (n.d.). *It's time to make learning personal.* Retrieved from http://personalizedlearningfoundation.org/id3.html.

Sizer, T. (1995). *Horace's hope: What works for the American high school.* Boston: Houghton Mifflin.

Sizer, T. (1997). *Horace's school: Redesigning the American high school.* Boston: Houghton Mifflin Harcourt.

Staveley-O'Carroll, S. (n.d.). *All MetWest grads accepted to four-year colleges* [Press release]. Providence, RI: Big Picture Learning.

Steinberg, A. (2000). *Forty-three valedictorians: Graduates of the Met talk about their learning.* Boston: Jobs for the Future. Retrieved from http://www.bigpicture.org/wp-content/uploads/2008/10/001018-jobs-for-the-future.pdf.

Vermont Department of Education. (2002). *High schools on the move: Renewing Vermont's commitment to quality secondary education.* Montpelier, VT: Author.

Washor, E., Arnold, K., & Mojkowski, C. (2009). Now what? Data beyond high school. *Educational Leadership, 66*(4), 60–64.

Index

CORWIN

A SAGE Company

The Corwin logo—a raven striding across an open book—represents the union of courage and learning. Corwin is committed to improving education for all learners by publishing books and other professional development resources for those serving the field of PreK–12 education. By providing practical, hands-on materials, Corwin continues to carry out the promise of its motto: **"Helping Educators Do Their Work Better."**